Hidden treasures

Works of art from Oxfordshire private collections

Hidden treasures

Catherine Whistler, Christopher White and Rosemary Baird

Exhibition sponsored by
Mercers, Solicitors, Henley-on-Thames and Reading

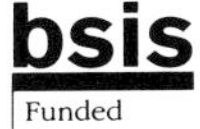

Ashmolean Museum Oxford 1993

First published to coincide with the exhibition at the Ashmolean
Museum, Oxford, 27 July – 17 October 1993

Mercers, Solicitors of Henley-on-Thames and Reading are an award
winner under the Business Sponsorship Incentive Scheme for their
support of the Ashmolean Museum's exhibition 'Hidden treasures'.
The BSIS is a Government scheme administered by the Association
for Business Sponsorship of the Arts.

British Library Cataloguing in Publications Data
A catalogue record for this book is available from the British Library

ISBN 1 85444 033 0

Cover illustrations
front: Jean-Baptiste Siméon Chardin *Le faiseur de châteaux de cartes*
catalogue no. 11
back: Joseph Mallord William Turner *View of the High Street, Oxford*
catalogue no. 60

Designed by Cole design unit, Reading
Set in Apollo by Meridian Phototypesetting Limited
Printed and bound in Great Britain by Cheney & Sons Limited,
Banbury, Oxfordshire

It is with especial pleasure that the Ashmolean presents an exhibition of paintings, drawings and sculpture from Oxfordshire collections. The show offers the visitor the opportunity to see a number of important and attractive works, which, with one exception, are not on view to the public. Without the generosity of the owners prepared to be without their possessions over much of the summer there would be no exhibition, and I would like to begin by expressing our warm gratitude to them.

The exhibition, which has been several years in the making, grew out of the like-minded wishes of several keen supporters of the Museum. Mrs Anne Heseltine, who had just taken on the chairmanship of our advisory committee for fundraising, was anxious, as part of the Campaign for Oxford, to increase the county's awareness of the Museum. Mr Martin Riley, the senior partner of Mercers, Solicitors of Henley-on-Thames, who is a long-standing Friend, wished to establish a closer contact between Henley and its surroundings with the Museum. He had thought of an exhibition drawn from local collections but limited to Venetian art. Mr Hugo Brunner who had a rather different theme for an exhibition in mind, good naturedly threw in his lot with the present exhibition. We were also fortunate to attract the participation of Mr James Miller, whose professional knowledge of the contents of local houses must be unrivalled. Dr Kenneth Garlick, a former Keeper of the Department of Western Art, also joined us and, in addition to writing a charming and personal introduction, was hardly less well informed about local collections. Dr Catherine Whistler served as curator of the exhibition; during her absence on sabbatical leave, Mrs Rosemary Baird stood in as an equally expert and efficient organiser. We are most grateful to them all for forming a highly professional and effective exhibition committee.

Unfortunately love of the Ashmolean by itself is not enough to realise such a venture, and given the Museum's current financial situation it was imperative to raise outside funds. Thanks to the efforts of both Martin Riley and Hugo Brunner, we are in a position to express our sincere gratitude to Messrs Mercers, whose contribution was matched by an equal sum from the Association of Business Sponsorship in the Arts, to the late Miss N.Q. Radcliffe-Platt, the PF Charitable Trust, the Barnsbury Charitable Trust and Mr Martyn Arbib for their generous donations, which apart from covering all the other costs of making an exhibition enabled us to publish this illustrated catalogue.

If we cannot claim to have identified a specifically Oxfordshire taste, we were surprised by the riches and variety of works of art contained within the city and the county. When I first arrived here, I was advised, as a potential museum acquisitor, to walk up and down the streets of North Oxford at dusk, when the lights in private houses were on but the curtains not yet drawn: peeping through the windows I would undoubtedly see, I was assured, a surprising wealth of possessions displayed in the rooms. The exhibition has not only proved the correctness of this advice, applied to a much wider catchment-area, but has meant that, along with other members of the committee, I was welcomed in at the front door by hospitable owners rather than being forced to creep surreptitiously across lawns and to trample on flower-beds, in constant danger of being spotted by a local policeman. And if we were struck by the wide scope of works in private possession, as the exhibition illustrates, we were also impressed by the range of those who collect or own collections. All, however, have one thing in common; their private enjoyment of their possessions. For over two months we are privileged to share their pleasure.

We are very grateful to Michael Dudley, the Ashmolean

Museum photographer, for his experience and expertise in providing excellent photographs of paintings often in difficult locations. For their assistance with the preparation of the exhibition and catalogue, Vivien Stchedroff, Brigid Cleaver and Rebecca Marles have been invaluable. We would also like to thank experts who have given generously of their time and talents, notably Mildred Archer, David Brown, Peter Cannon-Brookes, Tom Cross, John Ingamells, Lee Johnson, Anne Scottez-De Wambrechies, Nicholas Tromans, Nicholas Turner, Jon Whiteley, Linda Whiteley.

Measurements are given in centimetres, height before width. A single reference to the scholarly literature has been provided where known, either to a standard source or to a useful recent work which supercedes earlier references.

Christopher White
Director

Introduction

This exhibition is not intended as a lesson in art history, though many such a lesson could be based upon it. It is intended to bring together from private sources works of art of high quality which members of the public may enjoy independently, in isolation from their neighbours on the wall, and without reference to other works of the same period or the same school. You might call it a private exhibition. It is also a tribute to the private collector. It will be sad if the day ever comes when fine works of art are to be found only in museums and art galleries. Collecting is a natural human instinct and in this instance is a kind of life-blood for the circulation of painting and drawings and objets d'art ensuring that they move from home to home as a civilising and formative influence. Some have come to their owners by inheritance. Others have come by purchase, so revealing the taste of the collector. Adding to one's collection is by no means always a matter of money. It is a matter of experience and certainty, and serendipity plays a large part in it. Private owners are almost always generous when asked to lend to exhibitions. This event could not be a better example of that.

This is an exhibition to browse in, to visit, to go away and return to, without obligation to have guide-book or potted history in hand. Note-book, yes. Guide-book, no. It is always rewarding when browsing among pictures to decide which of them speak to you personally, which you would choose to live with and learn from. The results are sometimes surprising because the things of your choice do not always harmonise together. In my case I would in the first place select the Cézanne, *A Farmhouse among Trees,* with its elemental tree and branch forms set timelessly in space, an ideal, architectural landscape, rather like one of Piero della Francesca's ideal cities, empty, waiting for the advent of humanity. I would add the Vuillard, grey and white houses, light and air, timeless again, expressing a continuity of village life which in today's world has perhaps been lost for ever; then the still Chardin built up like the house of cards on the table by a thought process which carries over to the spectator; and finally William Turner of Oxford's watercolour of a path across a cornfield leading to an infinity, an absolution from the trivial activities of everyday life, opening to a larger activity of the mind.

In contrast to these because they are less intellectual – or perhaps the words should be 'less purified' – I would add to my list the Guardi and the Corot. Guardi's small Venetian scene, one of many of the kind he produced, is among the best of them. I think one may call Guardi a romantic although in his time the word was not in common usage. His romanticism is more evident in his use of paint than in his subject-matter which, after all, is the same as Canaletto's, and one could not conceivably call Canaletto a romantic. Guardi's application of paint is rich, lush, steeped in the deep colours that emerge in strong Italian sunlight. One can enjoy immoderately the rich modelling of the broken pediment over the door knocked into the wall of the churchyard, or the weeds on the church's rooftops. This is more redolent of the Italian inheritance than Canaletto's precise recordings, lively as they are. You get the same feeling, nearer to Guardi, from the *View of the Dolo on the Brenta* by Canaletto's nephew, Bellotto. Similarly Corot's *Landscape with Seated Figure by a Lake,* which reminds one of another late landscape by him which came to the Ashmolean with the Hock bequest in 1987. Corot's early landscapes have always been valued more highly than those of his later years. They have a direct and superbly painterly response to the French or Italian scenes which are before his eyes. His later landscapes are evocations rather than re-sponses. They relate in mood to literature, to classical pas-torals, Theocritus or Virgil. They are vague, sometimes weak, but at their best, as in this case, they re-create the classical idyll with a personal poetry. In a way too they are of the mood of the Samuel Palmer school. Calvert, had he developed further, might have painted something like this.

It is a difficult if not impossible task to introduce so varied an exhibition as this without hopping from picture to picture and drawing to drawing and subject to subject in a more than muddled manner. One can try to tackle it by period. For instance the years 1790–1830 throughout Europe cover the period now defined as 'romantic', and there are some splendid examples from that period here. Who would expect to find so vivid a late Goya 'hidden' in this county? Or a Delacroix? Or so dramatic a Francia as *The Parys Copper Mine in Anglesey*? Moreover there are four Turners, two oil and two watercolours and one Bonington, all of the first calibre. One of them is of the greatest interest in the context of the Ashmolean. *View of the High Street, Oxford* was painted by Turner around 1810 for James Wyatt, the print-dealer and frame-maker on the south side of the High, who later became a patron of the young Pre-Raphaelites. It was in his shop-window that Burne-Jones and Morris, as undergraduates, saw their first Pre-Raphaelite Brotherhood painting, Millais' *Return of the Dove to the Ark,* now in the Ashmolean. Turner's record of the High brings home to us the degra-dation which the motor-car has brought to this city and the loss of the once prevalent awareness as one walked around, that this is the home of a great centre of learning. It was painted at a time when the wearing of academic dress was customary. Today, alas, it is exceptional. The loss is self-inflicted. Turner took great trouble with this picture, paying unusual attention to Mr Wyatt's suggestions for alterations in detail. He later painted a companion, *Oxford from the Abingdon Road,* also owned privately but not in this county.

Among the English romantic portraitists Lawrence was the great name. We are fortunate to have been able to bor-row an example of his late, sophisticated style, the *Portrait of*

Mrs Benjamin Gott, the wife of a successful manufacturer and patron of the arts in Leeds. She is obviously a lady of money and fashion, but shrewd, quite a different breed from the London ladies of fashion whom Lawrence painted weighed down with satin and opulent jewellery, much more than Mrs Gott chooses to display. One would be careful not to risk the sharp edge of her tongue.

Three other portraits are exceptional. John Russell's portrait of *The Old Porter at the Royal Academy* gives the strength of an oil painting to a pastel. Porters of established institutions take great pride in their duties and this is transmitted here by associating the sitter with the casts from the antique in the background and the token which he holds up for all to see. It is a suave and proud portrait. In contrast the small portraits of his daughter, Lucy, by Ford Madox Brown and of Christina Rossetti by her brother, Dante Gabriel, are intense, eye-to-eye, and loving. They would probably have surprised Russell. He would have found them eye-openers.

The collecting of drawings has a history going back at least to the sixteenth century when Giorgio Vasari formed his *Libro dei Disegni.* It can easily become an obsession. The wealth of survival of drawings and sketches in private hands is astonishing when one realises how much has already accumulated in the great print rooms of Europe and America. The drawings here are such as any print room would be proud to own, notably the Palma Giovane, the Tiepolos, the Boucher, and, if one can count watercolour as drawing, the Sandby.

Finally the exhibition tumbles into the twentieth century with Munnings' *Fancy Dress Party: the Chelsea Arts Club* of 1901 and rushes forward as if it does not quite know what it is doing or where it is going, to Max Beerbohm's caricature of Lord Berners of 1923, coming to a halt in 1945 with Henry Lamb's *Four Ladies leaving Coombe Bisset Church.* The group includes Miss Edith Olivier, a personality and a lady of letters, a close friend of Rex Whistler and Siegfried Sassoon. Her memoir, *Without knowing Mr Walkley,* is a now almost forgotten charmer of the thirties.

It is a very English ending.

I have scarcely mentioned the Dutch and Flemish paintings which include a fine church interior by Anthonie de Lorme, a good Teniers in an excellent state of conservation, and a somewhat daunting Honthorst. I have not mentioned sculpture. Space begins to run out. But there is nothing in the exhibition which is below standard. Let us hope that the public flocks to see it.

Kenneth Garlick

The following illustrations are reproduced in colour:

Plate 3	page 18
Plate 9	page 19
Plate 13	page 22
Plate 14	page 23
Plate 19	page 26
Plate 32	page 26
Plate 36	page 30
Plate 38	page 22
Plate 55	page 31
Plate 69	page 27

Cover illustrations – numbers 11 and 60

1 Balthasar van der Ast (c.1590–1656) *Still-life*
Oil on panel. 18 : 32.5. Signed: *B.van der Ast*

The artist, a specialist in still-life painting, was a follower and probably a pupil of Abraham Bosschaert. The painting combines his principal three subjects, flowers, fruit and shells. He may well have made his own collection of shells, often not from Europe.

2 Sir Max Beerbohm (1872–1956) *Lord Berners, making more Sweetness than Violence*
Watercolour over pencil. 32.5 : 20. Signed: *Max 1923*

Sir Gerald Hugh Tyrwhitt-Wilson, 14th Lord Berners (1883–1950), is the subject of this caricature, which was exhibited at the Leicester Galleries, 1923, and reproduced in *Things New and Old*, 1923. Lord Berners – diplomat, composer, novelist, painter – lived at Faringdon House and was perhaps best known for his lively wit and mischievous humour.

Lit.: R.Hart-Davis, *A Catalogue of the Caricatures of Max Beerbohm* (London, 1972), no. 142.

3 Bernardo Bellotto (1721–1780) *View of Dolo on the Brenta Canal*
Oil on canvas. 60 : 94 (sight)

The Brenta Canal was the gateway to Venice from the north, and its shores were lined with villas, country retreats for the Venetian nobility. The source for Bellotto's view must have been the painting by his uncle, Canaletto, which is in the Ashmolean Museum (A146): Canaletto also made some etchings of views of Dolo.

Lit.: S.Kozakiewicz, *Bernardo Bellotto* (London, 1972), no. 29.

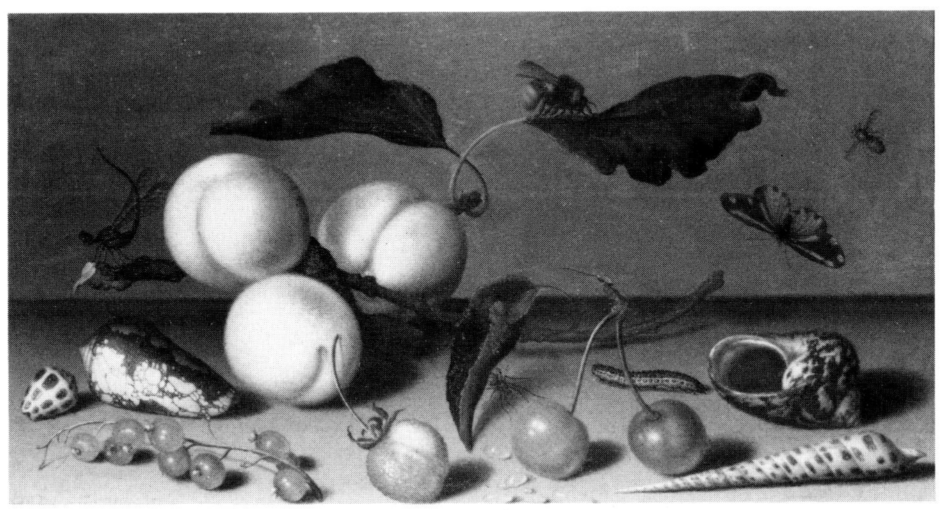

1

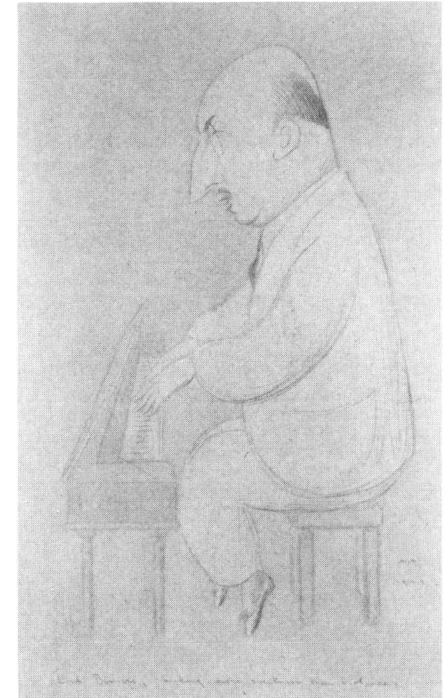

2

4 Ascribed to Louis-Leopold Boilly (1761–1845) *Standing Figure of a Woman*
Charcoal and white chalk on blue paper. 36 : 27.8
This charming sheet has an old attribution to Boilly, recently rejected by A. Scottez. The main study, essentially of the fall of the drapery, dates from the 1790s on the evidence of costume, and may be connected with a figure in a genre or narrative scene. A rough sketch of a seated woman is in the upper left on the sheet, put down probably as an afterthought, perhaps with a portrait in mind.

5 Bolognese school *c.*1590–1600 *St. John the Evangelist and St. Francis; The Mourning Virgin and Mary Magdalen*
Oil on panel. 33 : 17 each

These are clearly fragments of a larger painting of the *Crucifixion with Saints,* which was probably a private devotional work. The sensitively painted figures and the attention to the expression of emotion, are reminiscent of the early work of Guido Reni, for example his *Coronation of the Virgin with Four Saints* (Bologna, Pinacoteca Nazionale). The painting may be by an artist in his circle, or that of his first teacher Denys Calvaert.

6 Richard Parkes Bonington (1802–1828) *Study of the Normandy Coast*
Oil on canvas. 21.5 : 34
Bonington began painting his beach scenes in oils from 1824, presumably hoping to sell them through the intimate market of his

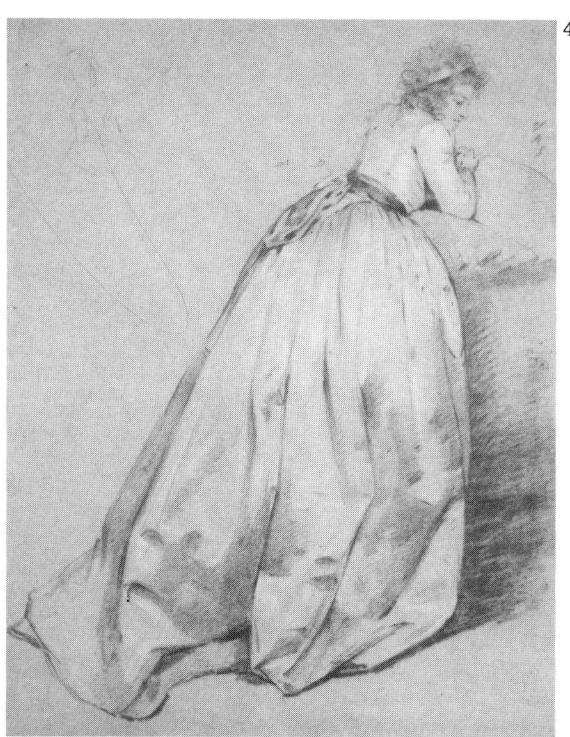

4

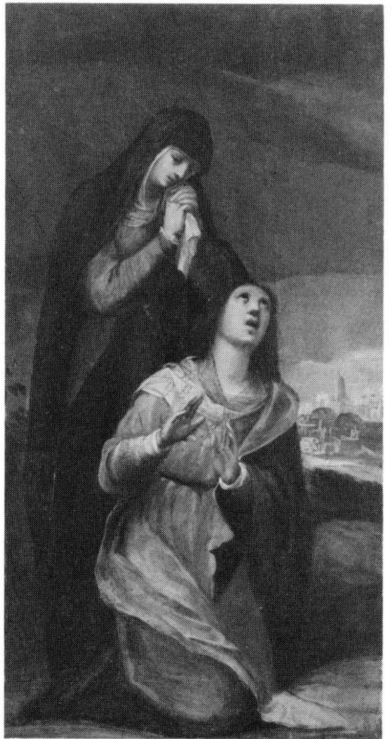

5a

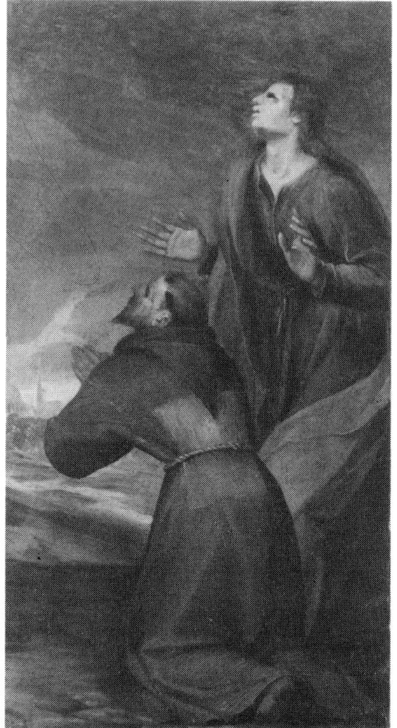

5b

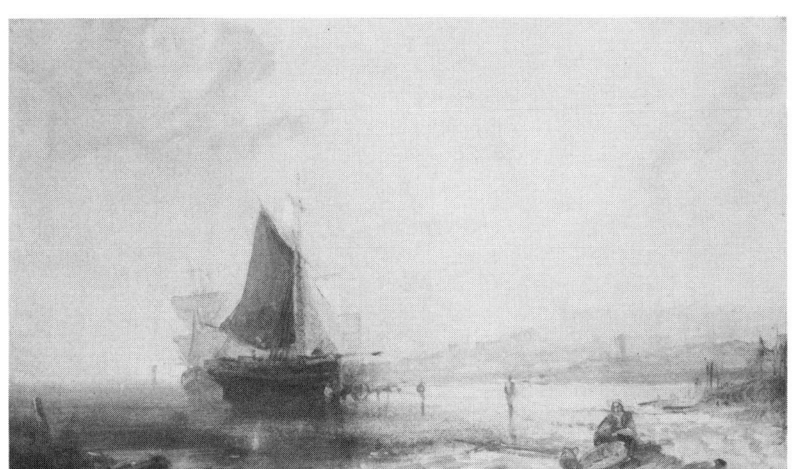

6

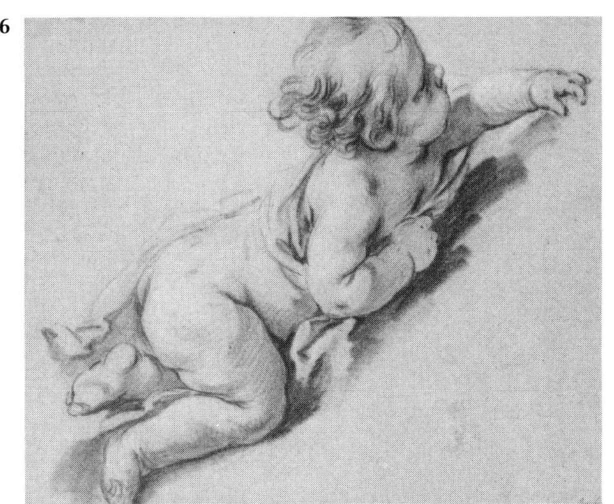

7

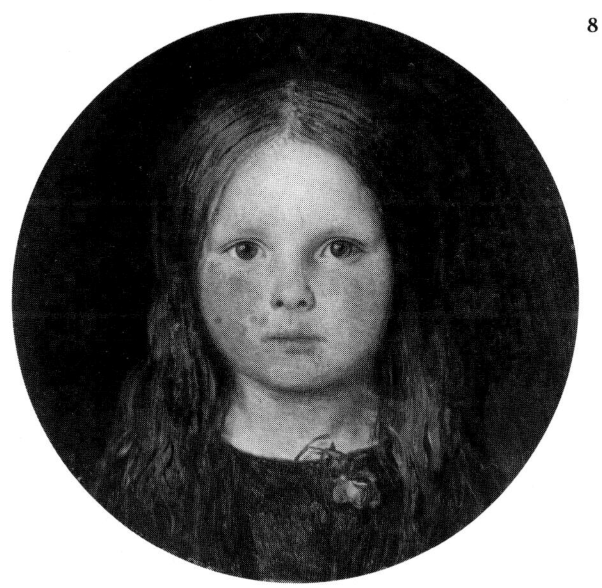

8

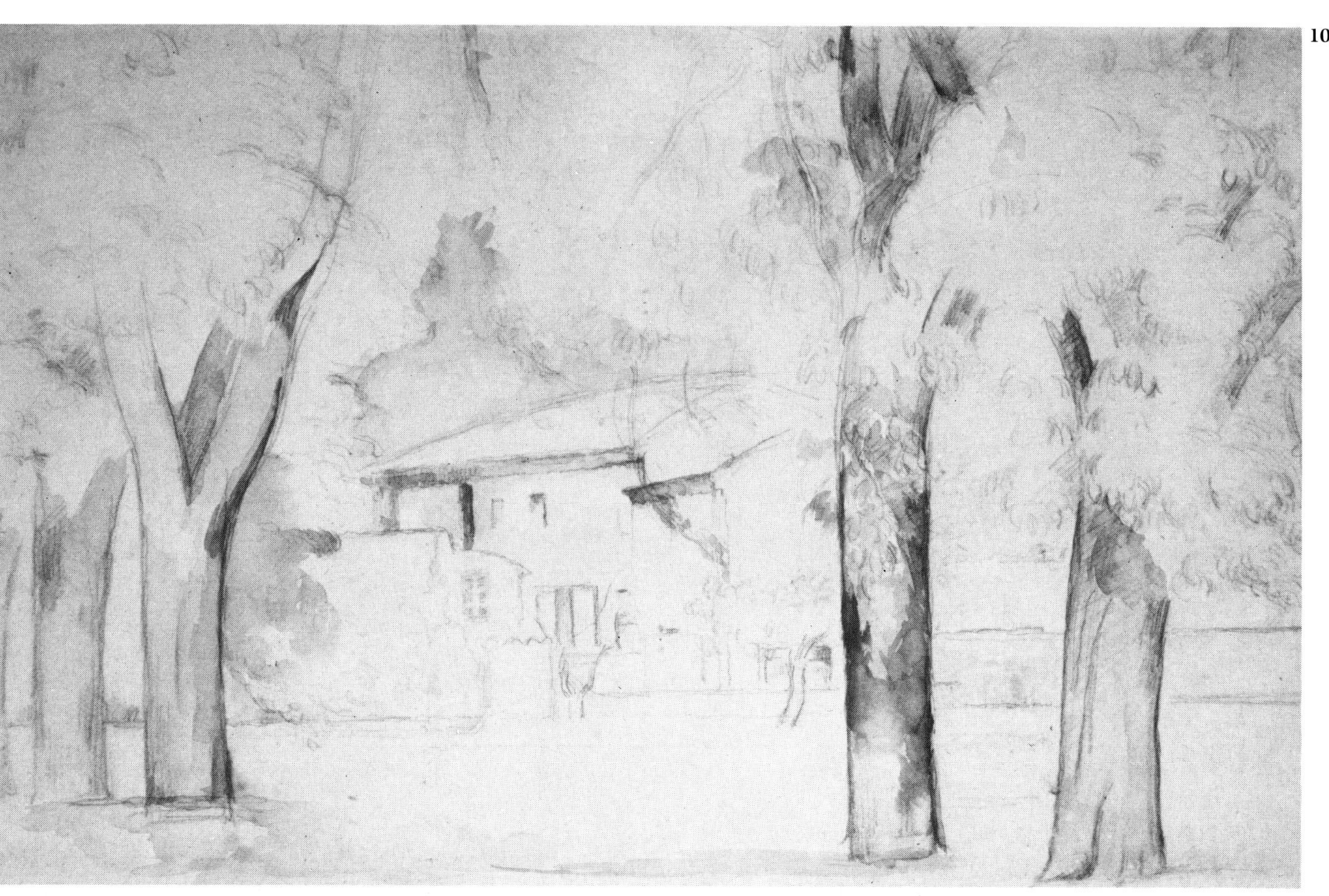

circle of admirers. This picture probably dates from his freer style of 1825–26. Bonington painted many such beach sketches, often with similar composition, and despite his enthusiasm for open-air painting, often produced them in the studio.

7 François Boucher (1703–1770) *Study of a Putto*
Black chalk heightened with white, with some grey wash, on buff paper. 24.3 : 29
This lively study is comparable with a drawing in the British Museum, a study for the figure of Cupid in *L'Amour Desarmé* in the Hearst Collection, New York of 1751.
Lit.: A. Ananoff, *François Boucher*, II, (Lausanne and Paris, 1976), no.375/12, Fig.1096.

8 Ford Madox Brown (1821–1893) *Portrait of the Artist's Daughter, Lucy*
Oil on cardboard. Roundel, 15.2 diameter

This is probably the painting recorded in the artist's diary for August-September 1849: three sittings were needed for this sharply focussed image of a serious little child. Lucy (1843–94) later married William Michael Rossetti, the brother of Dante Gabriel.
Lit.: Exhibition catalogue, *The Pre-Raphaelites* (Tate Gallery, London, 1984), no. 21.

9 Antonio Canal, called Canaletto (1697–1768) *Westminster Bridge, with Lambeth Palace in the Distance*
Oil on canvas. 47 : 74.5
Painted in 1754 for Thomas Hollis, one of Canaletto's most important patrons in England, this panoramic view, with its lively foreground details, gives London the air of a Venetian *veduta*. Westminster Bridge, completed in 1746, is shown under repair: some work took place in 1748–49, and there were further repairs in 1752. Canaletto also painted the bridge in the course of construction in

12

15

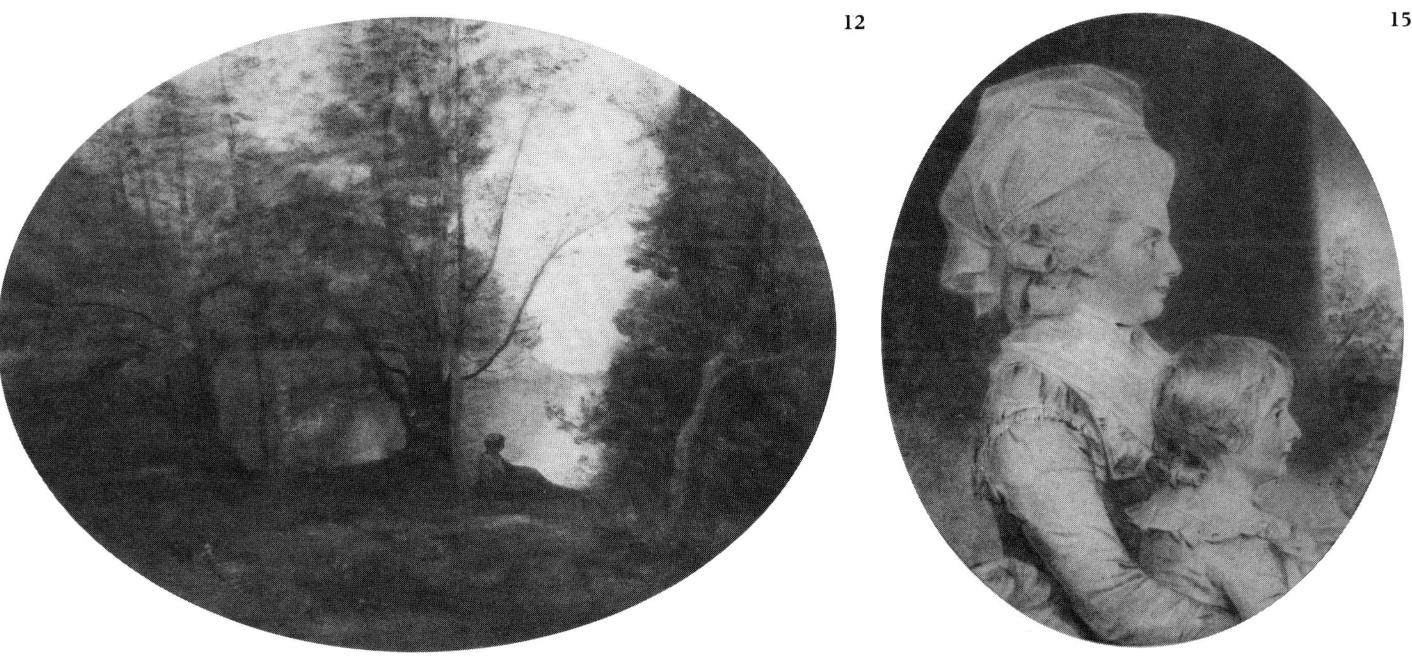

1746 (Constable no., 434) and made drawings of the bridge during the repair work (e.g. Constable no. 751).

Lit.: W.G.Constable and J.Links, *Canaletto* 2nd ed. (Oxford, 1989), no.437b and p.738.

10 Paul Cézanne (1839–1906) *Landscape: a Farmhouse among Trees*
Watercolour over graphite. 30.5 : 46.5 (sight)
This seems identical with the work published by Rewald, *La Ferme du Jas de Bouffan* of *c*.1880, known to him only from a photograph. In his paintings Cézanne had started to evolve his 'constructive' stroke, or square and diagonal brushwork by the late 1870s, but realised this could not be transferred to paper for watercolours.

Lit.: J. Rewald, *Paul Cézanne. The Watercolours* (London, 1983), no.114.

11 Jean-Baptiste Siméon Chardin (1699–1779) *Le faiseur de châteaux de cartes*
Oil on canvas. 76 : 99. Signed: J.B. Chardin
Probably exhibited at the Paris Salon of 1735, this is the first of a number of versions of this subject by Chardin (note the visible alterations to the hat and elsewhere made by the artist as he worked on the canvas). The scene is a naturalistic depiction of a boy with a favourite game, while it also has symbolic resonance.

Lit.: Exhibition catalogue, *The Treasure Houses of Britain* (National Gallery, Washington, 1985), no.152.

12 Jean-Baptiste Camille Corot (1796–1875) *Landscape with a Seated Figure by a Lake*
Oil on canvas. 52.5 : 39.5

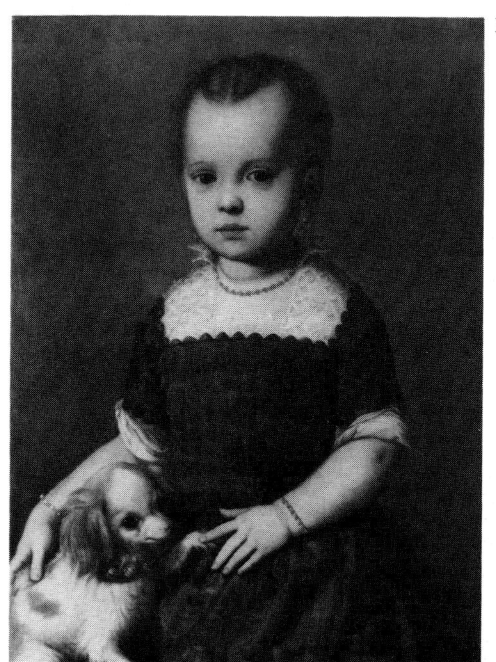

16

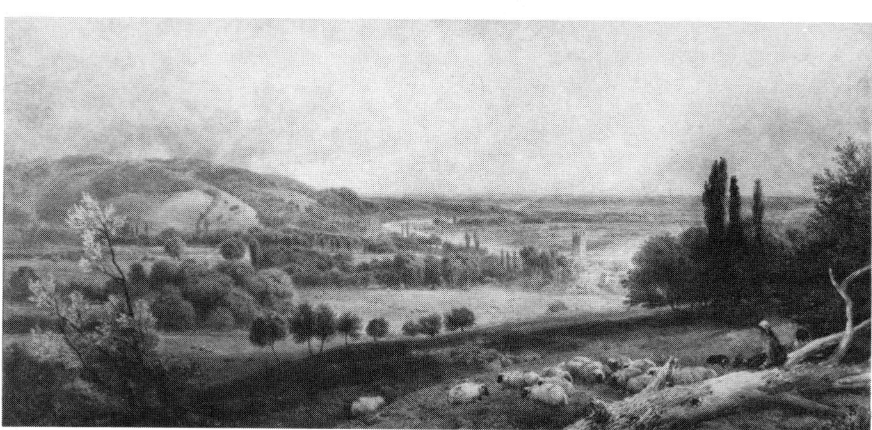

17

This tranquil landscape is extremely close to a small oval published by Robaut, *Solitude*, which was painted in 1851. Corot used this *plein air* study as the basis of a larger composition of 1866 which he showed at the Salon that year.

    Lit.: A.Robaut, *L'Oeuvre de Corot. Catalogue Raisonné*, 4 vols. (Paris, 1905), no.844.

13 Edgar Degas (1834–1917) *Figures in an Interior (Study for Le Viol)*
    Oil on canvas. 34 : 20

A study for the enigmatic painting called *Interior*, but also known as *The Rape*, probably of *c.*1868–69, now in the Philadelphia Museum of Art, this canvas shows Degas at an early stage of the composition. The final painting depicts a bearded mean, and a seated woman in *déshabillé* in a bedroom, suggesting that Degas was exploring an alternative idea for the scene. Amongst various sug-gestions as to the meaning of the painting – which Degas doubtless intended to be ambiguous – is that it might have been inspired by an episode from Zola's novel, *Thérèse Raquin* of 1867.

    Lit.: Exhibition catalogue, J. Sutherland Boggs et al, *Degas* (Grand Palais, Paris, National Gallery of Canada, Ottawa, and Metropolitan Museum, New York, 1988–89), under no.84.

14 Eugène Delacroix (1798–1863) *Tiger Hunt*
    Gouache over graphite. 31.5 : 24.5

Delacroix made a number of studies in the 1820s after the lion and tiger hunting scenes of Rubens, an artist he greatly admired. He was also able to study wild animals at the Jardin des Plantes in Paris. On stylistic grounds, this gouache is likely to date from *c.*1824–26 rather than from 1833, as Robaut states, after Delacroix had visited Morocco.

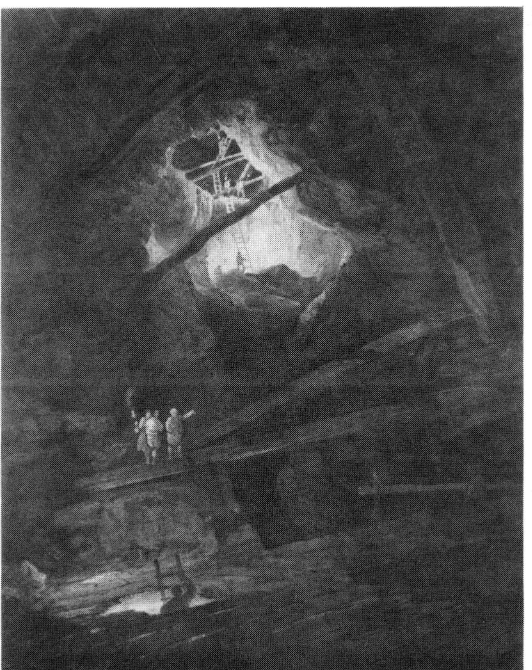

18

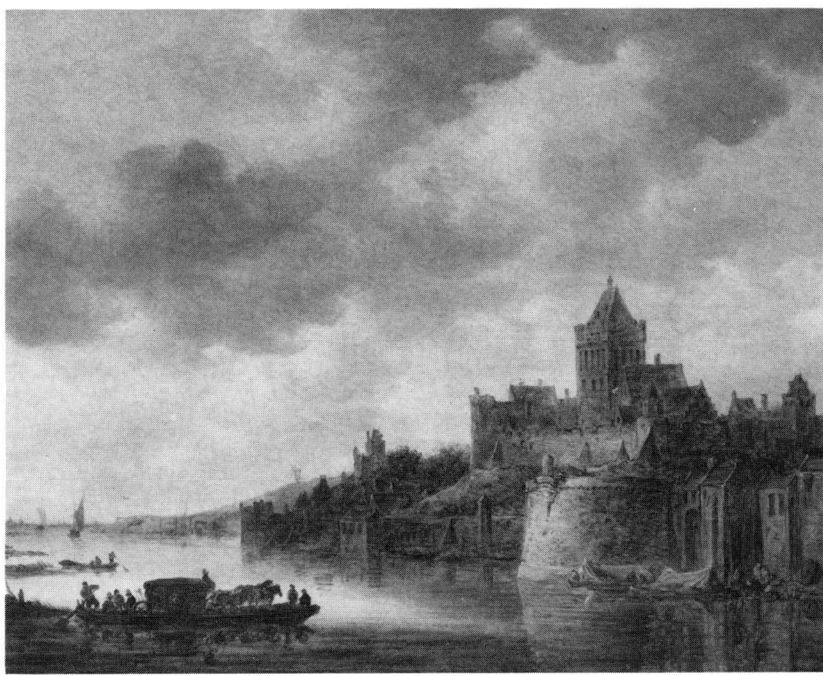

20

Lit.: A. Robaut, *L'Oeuvre Complet de Eugène Delacroix* (Paris, 1885), p.130, no. 485.

15 John Downman (c.1850–1824) *Mrs Blount of Mapledurham with her Daughter Mary Eugenia*
Black chalk and coloured chalks on buff paper. Oval 22 : 18.5.
Inscribed: J.Downman/pinx.t/17??
John Downman was an elegant portraitist in chalk and watercolour whose images have a distinctive naive prettiness. An old label on the frame identifies the sitters: Mary Eugenia Blount married Charles Stonor of Stonor (1737–1781). Their grandson Thomas became 3rd Lord Camoys.

16 Florentine School, late sixteenth century *Portrait of a Girl with a Dog*
Oil on canvas. 70.8 : 47.2
The charming sitter has not been identified. From the evidence of her costume, the painting can be dated to *c.*1570. Clearly the portrait is the work of an accomplished portrait painter: an attribution to Santi di Tito has recently been suggested.
Lit.: Catalogue, *The Loyd Collection* (1991), no.26.

17 Myles Birket Foster (1825–1899) *View of Henley*
Watercolour. 34:71. Signed with monogram.
Myles Birket Foster came from the North of England and first trained

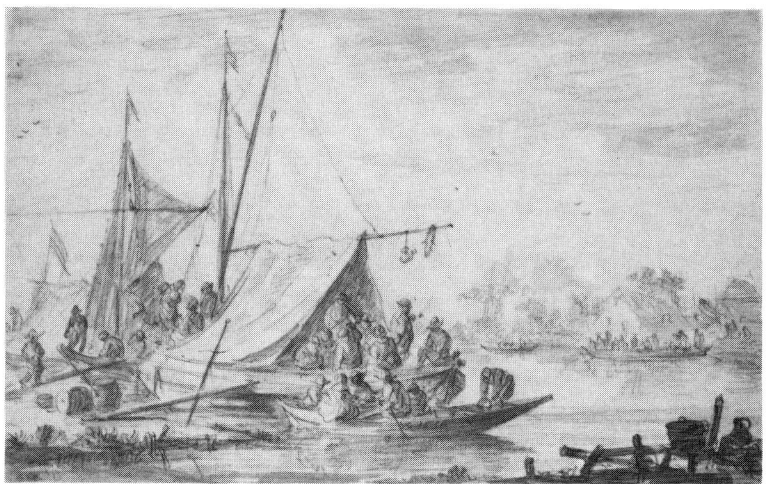

21

22

as a wood engraver. The stipple effect so often recognisable in his watercolours can be traced to this background. He invariably chose to paint peaceful scenes from the countryside, showing nothing of the influence of the Industrial Revolution.

Lit.: Exhibition catalogue, *British Watercolours and Drawings from Rowlandson to Riley* (The Royal Scottish Academy, 1982), no.77.

18 François Louis Thomas Francia (1772–1839) *The Parys Copper Mine in Anglesey*

Watercolour and bodycolour over black chalk. 510 : 400
Francia's dark tonalities and subtle use of colour are eminently suited to his subject, the copper mines on Parys Mountain which had opened in 1768. This is a striking example of one kind of response to the industrial landscape, where the sheer depth and darkness of the mine, and the dwarfing of the human figures evoke a mood of fear and near-reverence. A companion view of *c.*1809 is in the Elton Collection, Ironbridge Gorge Museum Trust: Francia shows the top of the mine, with the copper ore being hoisted up.

19 Francisco de Goya y Lucientes (1746–1828) *Head of a Young Woman*

Oil on canvas. 42 : 31. Dated on the verso: *1827*
One of Goya's last paintings, this belongs, together with the celebrated *Milkmaid of Bordeaux* (in the Museo del Prado, Madrid) to a small group of richly executed portraits and fanciful heads. There is a companion piece in a private collection showing an old bearded man in hooded cloak. The subjects have been traditionally identi-

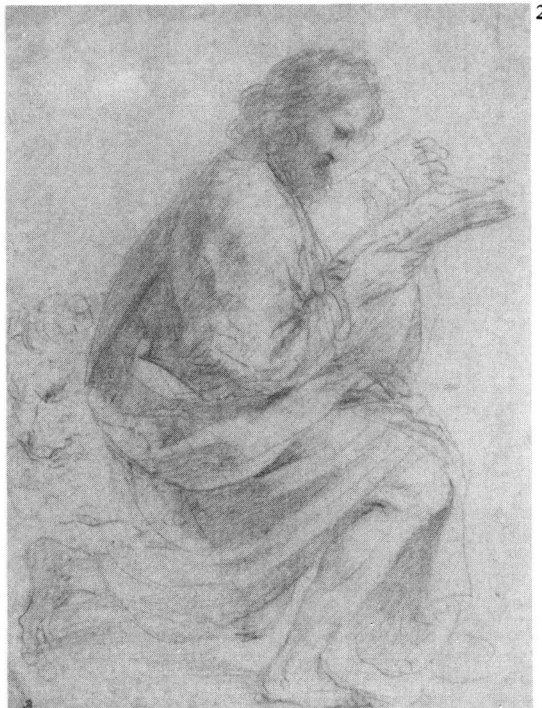

23

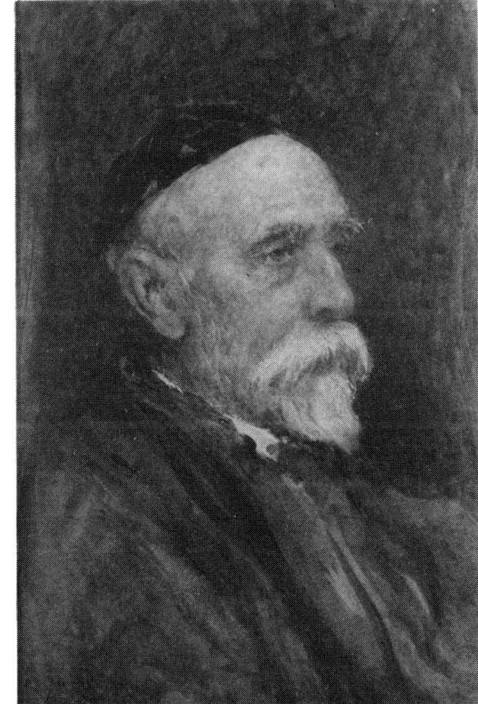

24

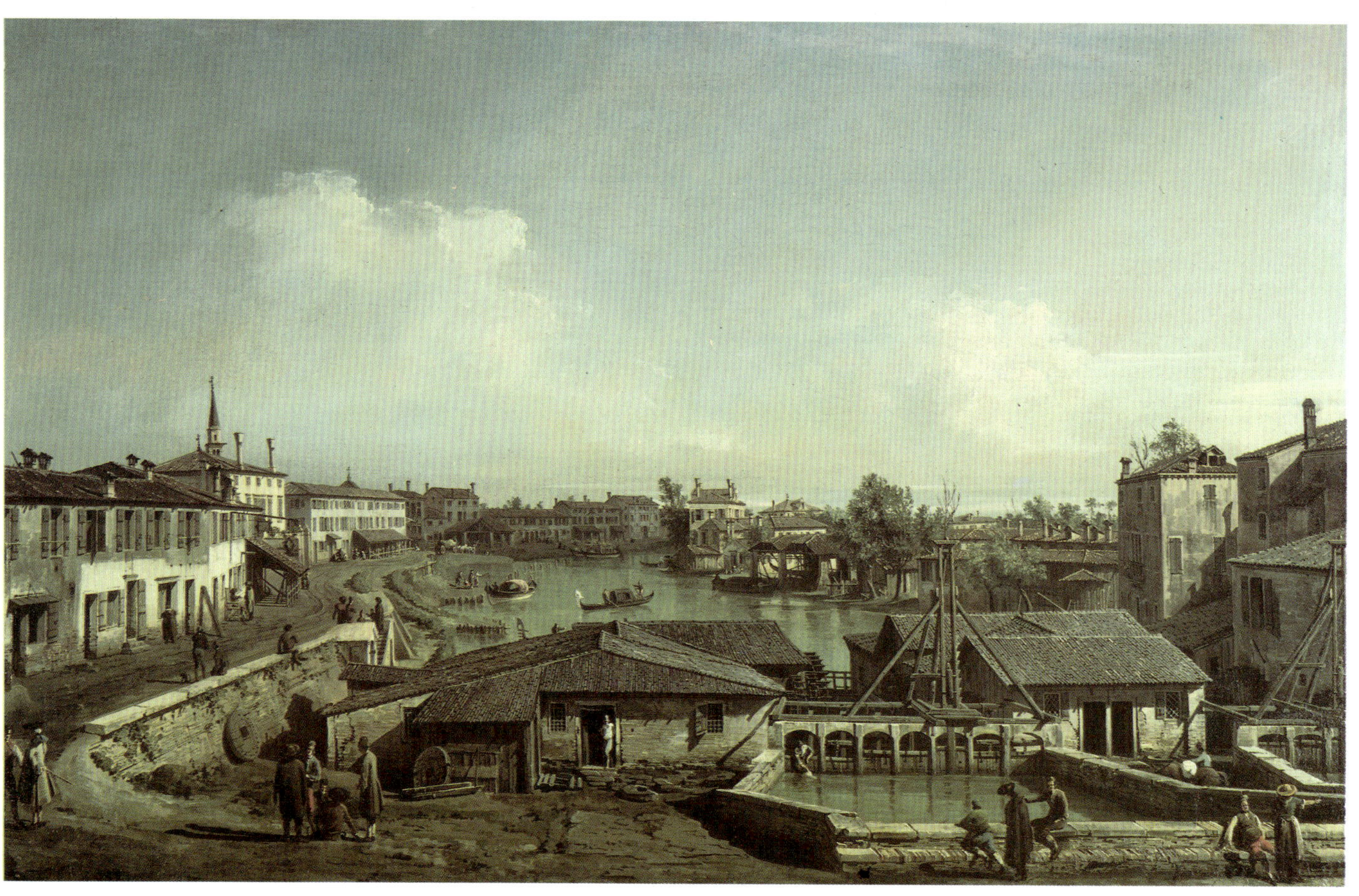

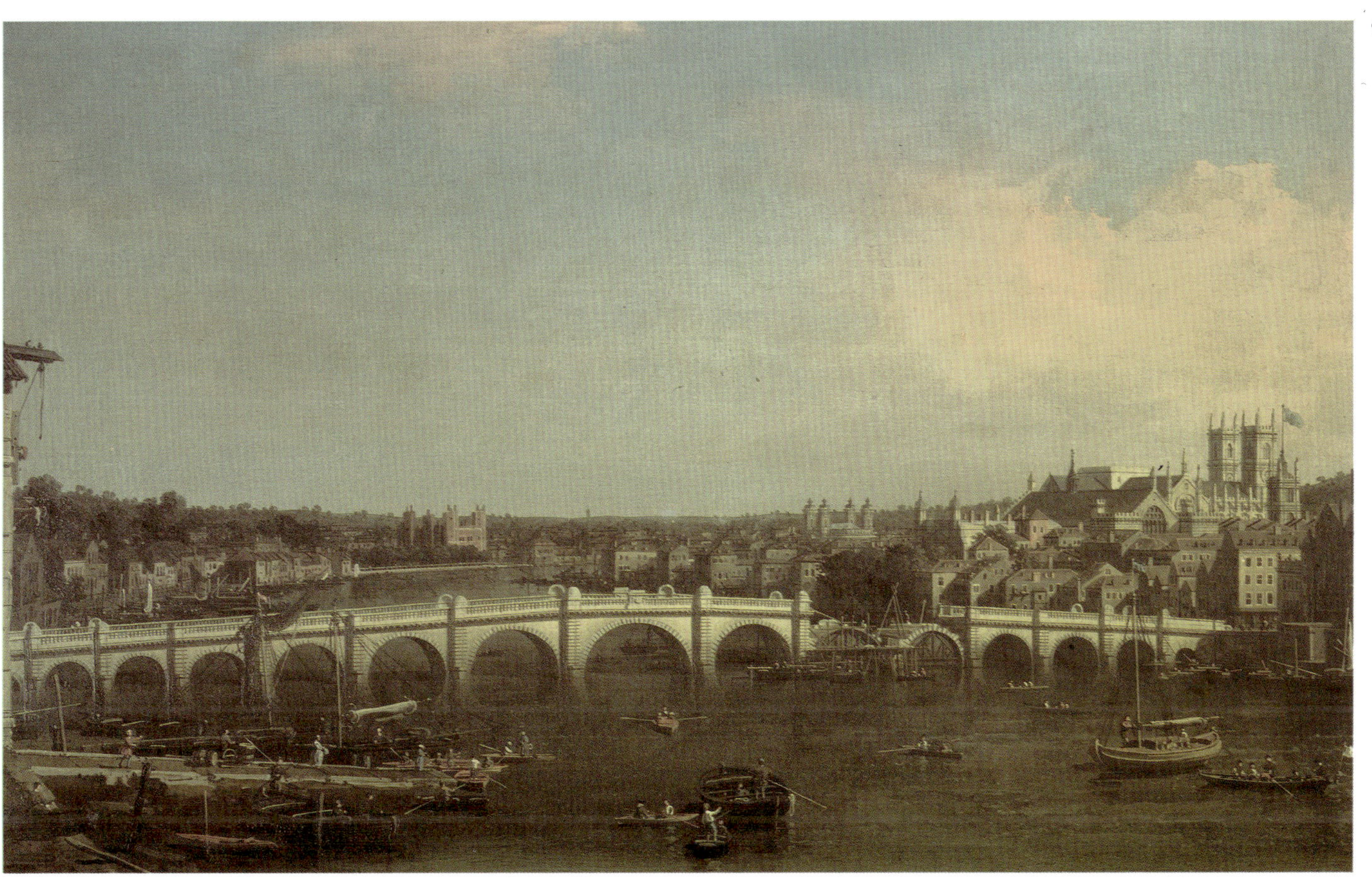

fied as a monk and a nun; both come from the collection of the Infante Don Sebastian de Borbon.

Lit.: P. Gassier and J. Wilson, *Goya, His Life and Work* (London, 1971), no.1668.

20 Jan van Goyen (1596–1656) *Nijmegen Castle seen from the River*
Oil on panel. 44.5 : 53.5. Signed and dated: *J. van Goyen 1646*
Nijmegen on the river Rijn, with the massive Valkhof towering above the town on the horizon, was a favourite theme of the artist from 1633 onwards. He tended to portray the subject from the same viewpoint, usually with a laden ferry-boat on the left; the present work is a close variation of another panel of the same date.

Lit.: H.-U. Beck, *Jan van Goyen 1596–1656*, II (Amsterdam, 1973), no.360.

21 Jan van Goyen (1596–1656) *Boats on a River*
Black chalk and brown wash. 17 : 27. Signed with monogram and dated: *VG 1651*
A tent has been erected on the nearest boat. The artist produced a large number of studies of river scenes throughout Holland and during 1650/1 made a sketching tour up the Rhine as far as Cleves.

Lit.: H.-U. Beck, *Jan van Goyen 1596–1656*, III (Doornspijk, 1987), no.268.

22 Francesco Guardi (1712–1793) *A Venetian Scene*
Oil on canvas. 55.5 : 41.6
Guardi made a speciality of these picturesque, sketchily painted scenes, sometimes including well-known or typical Venetian buildings – here an unidentifiable Gothic church – and colourful characters such as the dice-players. The picture was painted late in his career; a related drawing is in the Metropolitan Museum, New York.

Lit.: Catalogue, *The Loyd Collection* (1991), no.29.

23 Giovanni Francesco Barbieri, il Guercino (1591–1666) *St. Mark*
Red chalk on buff paper. 23.2 : 17.5 (sight)
The saintly figure with the attributes of a lion and a book could be identified as St. Mark or St. Jerome. Nicholas Turner suggested a date of the late 1650s or early 1660s, and pointed out that the pose is similar, although in reverse, to that of St. Bartholomew in an altarpiece in the Palazzo Rosso in Genoa, *c.*1651. No.23 comes from the important collection of John Bouverie (*c.*1722–50), who acquired several hundred Guercino drawings from the Gennari family.

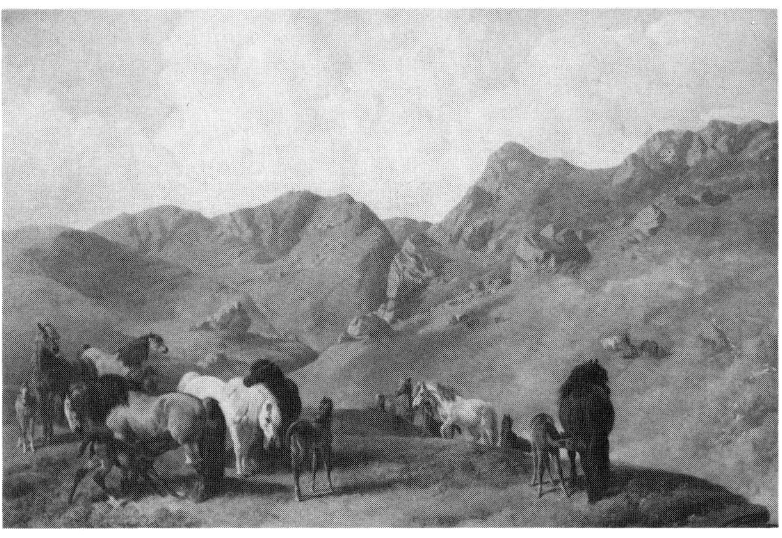

25

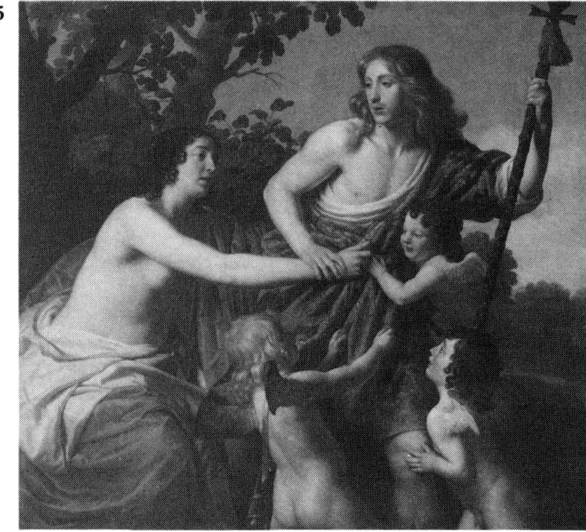

26

24 Sir Hubert von Herkomer (1849–1914) *Portrait of G.F. Watts (1817–1904)*

Watercolour and bodycolour on paper. 16.5 : 11 (sight)

The sitter was not only a portrait painter and sculptor but also an artist who sought to revive the tradition of grand-scale history painting. He achieved acclaim late in his career. Herkomer was equally virtuoso, writing music and opera as well as painting portraits of leading writers, artists and politicians of late Victorian England. This sensitive portrait shows the elderly Watts in a thoughtful mood. It seems to be a version of the watercolour exhibited at the Royal Watercolour Society in 1879, inscribed *To my friend G.F. Watts.*

Lit.: see A.L. Baldry, *Hubert von Herkomer* (London, 1901), facing p.58 and p.130.

25 John Frederick Herring (1795–1865) *'The Repose': Welsh Ponies in a Mountain Landscape*

Oil on canvas. 59.5 : 90. Signed and dated: 1854

The Repose and its pair *The Alarm* show a herd of ponies at first peacefully grazing and then in wild flight from a party of men appearing in the distance. The landscape mirrors the change in tempo, as the towering Cumulus clouds break. The background was painted by Henry Bright who often collaborated with Herring.

Lit.: O. Beckett, *J.F. Herring & Sons* (London, 1981), no.259.

26 Gerard van Honthorst (1590–1656) *Venus and Adonis*

Oil on canvas. 147 : 160. Signed and dated: *1641*

The mythological subject in a pastoral vein continues the convention established by Honthorst in his large painting at Hampton

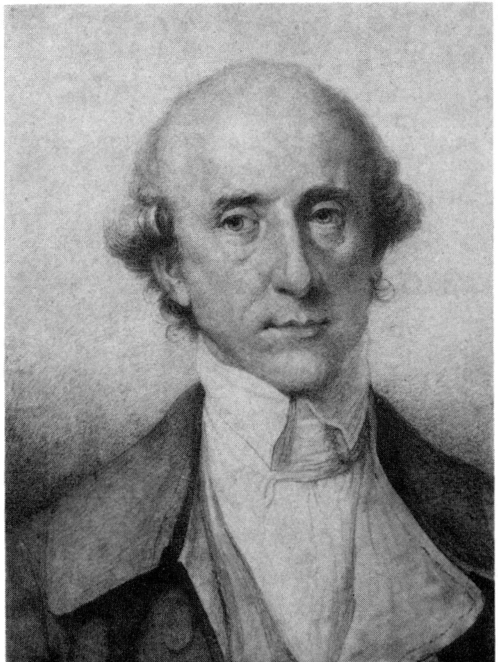

27

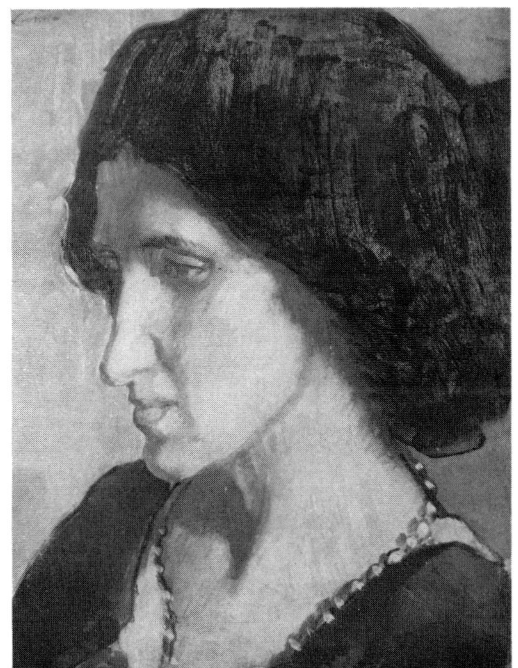

28

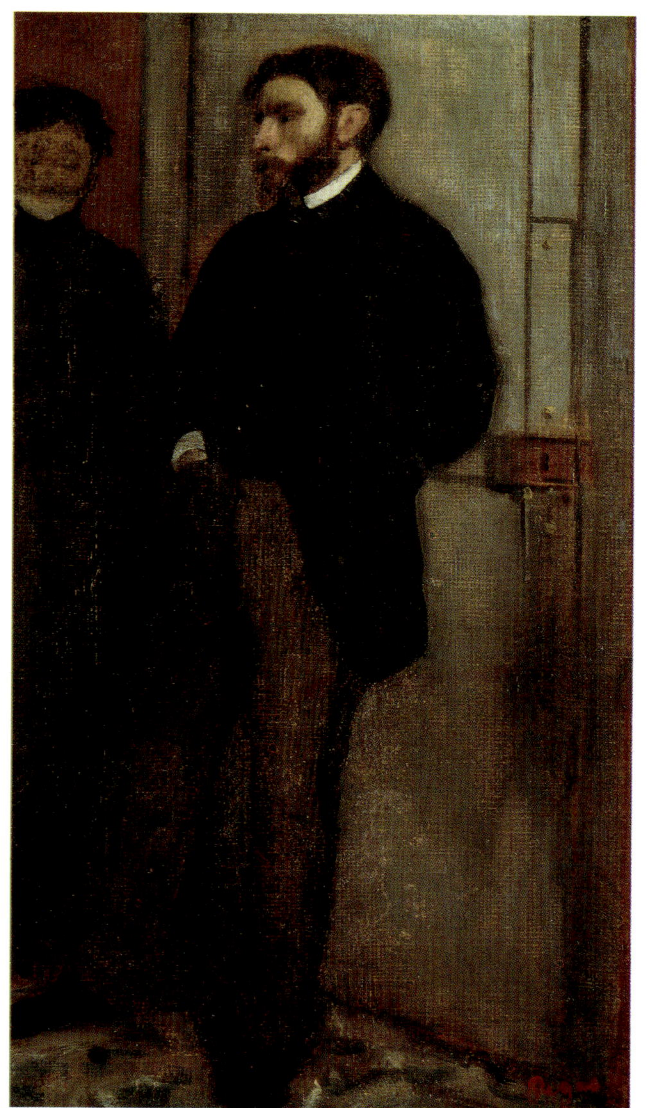

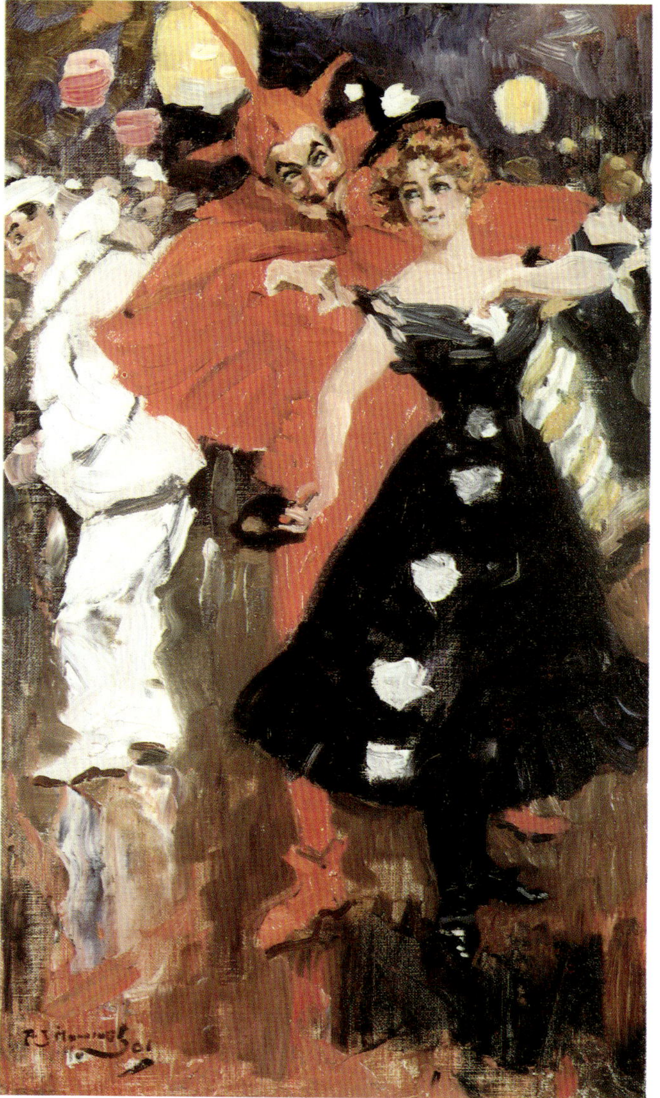

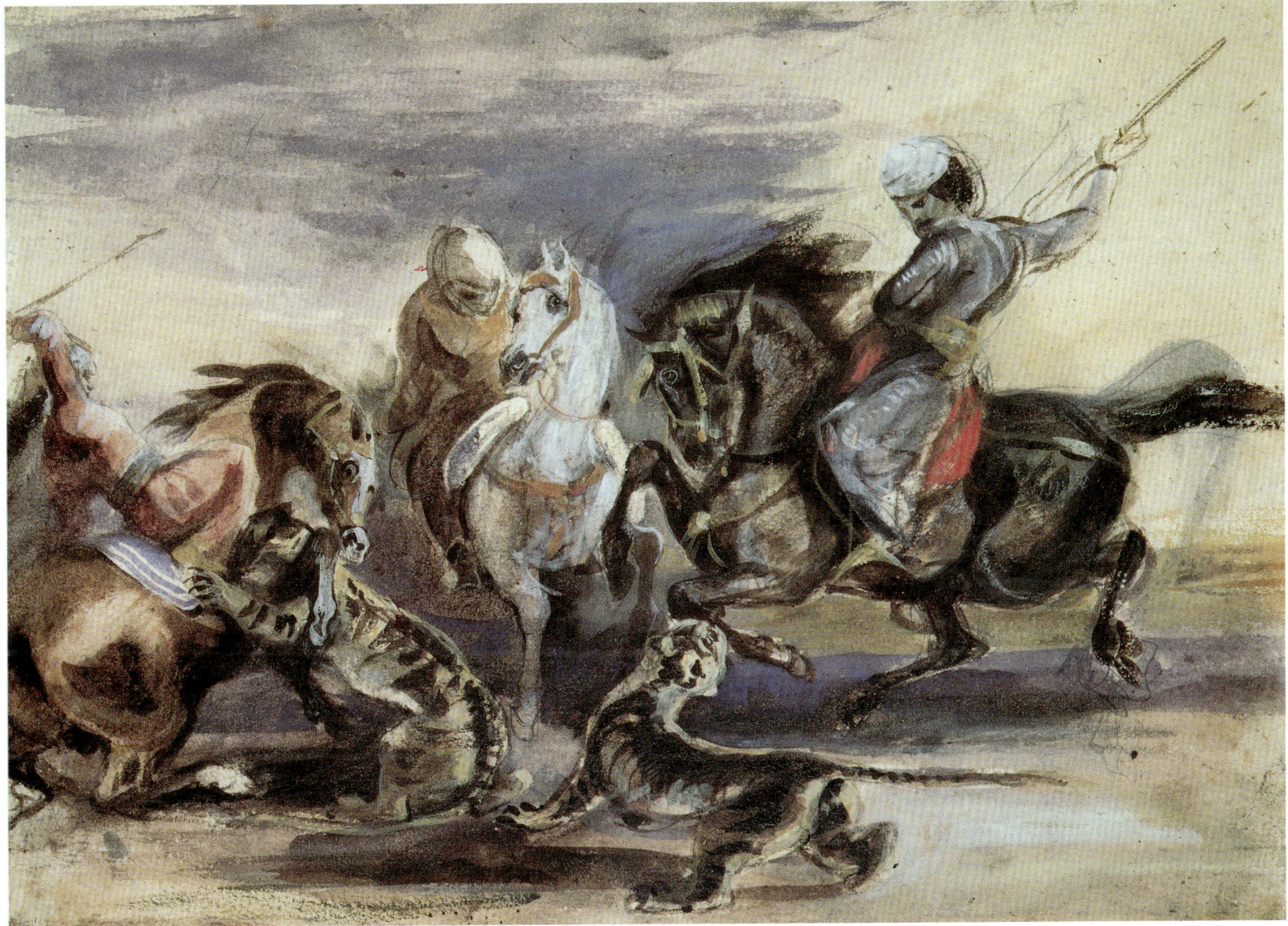

Court, which he executed when in England at the behest of the Duke of Buckingham in 1628. At the time that this later picture was painted, Honthorst was largely at the Hague and was Official Painter to Frederick Henry, Prince of Orange.

Lent by National Westminster Bank plc.

27 Ozias Humphrey (1742–1810) *Warren Hastings (1732–1818)*
Black, red and white chalks on off-white paper. 42 : 30.3
Warren Hastings was Governor General of India from 1773. He initiated vast reforms in the administration of justice and the collection of taxes, also rooting out corruption. His vigorous campaigns against the Mahrattas led to the supremacy of the British in India. The attribution of this drawing remains uncertain. There is a painting of Warren Hastings by Ozias Humphrey in the Victoria & Albert Museum.

28 Henry Lamb RA (1883–1960) *Lady Ottoline Morrell (1873–1938)*
Oil on panel. 23.5 : 18. Signed: *Lamb*
Lady Ottoline was a formidable and eccentric patron of early twentieth-century avant garde artists. She wore flamboyant and idiosyncratic clothes and entertained on a lavish scale, most notably members of the Bloomsbury Group. Ottoline and her husband Philip used Peppard Cottage, near Henley-on-Thames, as a country retreat before moving to Garsington. Lamb fell in love with her in the Spring of 1910, and took lodgings in the Dog Inn while working in a studio in her house. In the initial stage of their relationship he did several drawings of her, as well as beginning a full length portrait of her in 1911. This small panel shows his usual tendency to flatter and yet emphasise her pronounced features and individuality.

29

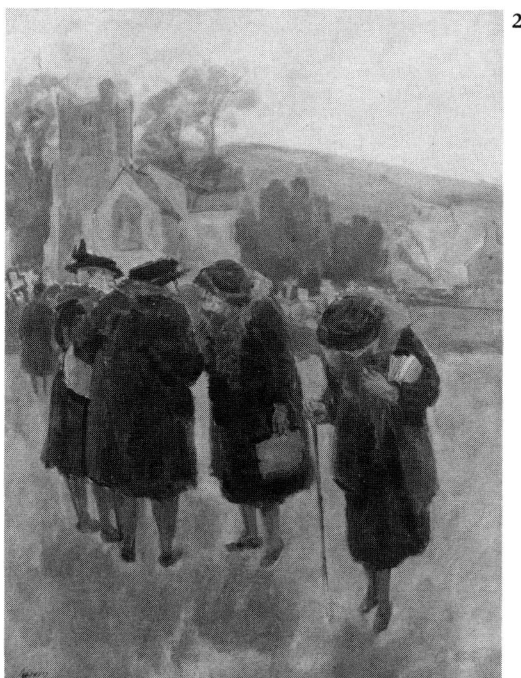

30

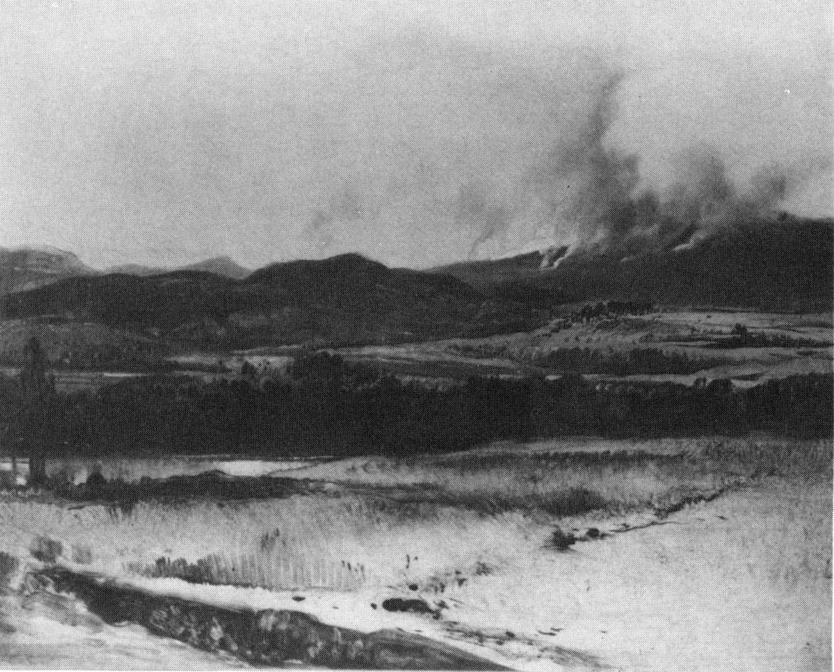

29 Henry Lamb RA (1883–1960) *Four Ladies leaving Coombe Bisset Church*

Oil on board. 45 : 34.5 (sight). Signed: *Lamb/45*

Coombe Bisset, a village west of Salisbury, was the home of Lamb and his wife Pansy Pakenham from their marriage in 1928 until his death in 1960. There they were visited by many of the fashionable literati of the day. Lamb often painted scenes around the village. This one shows from the right, Miss Edith Olivier, the Dowager Lady Radnor, Miss Stevenson and one unidentified lady. It was exhibited at the Leicester Galleries, Oct. 1945, no.32, as 'Witches Sabbath'.

30 Sir Edwin Henry Landseer (1802–73) *A Moorland Landscape*

Oil on board. 19 : 24

The artist first visited the Highlands in 1824, returning annually to an area which had recently become fashionable, with wealthy young aristocrats taking lodges for the shooting, fishing and stalking every autumn. Landseer was one of the first painters to give expression to the romance of the Scottish hills. The painting dates from 1825–35. In the distance can be seen the burning of the heather, clearing the way for the new shoots on which the young grouse will feed. There are similar Highland sketches in the Yale Center for British Art.

Lit.: Catalogue, *The Loyd Collection* (1991), no.38.

31 Marcellus Laroon (*c*.1648/49–1701/2) *Cries of the City of London*

An album of drawings in pencil, grey and brown ink and wash.

Illustrated: *A Merry New Song.* 22.2 : 16

Laroon, an assistant to Kneller, was a portraitist and engraver. His *Cryes of the City of London*, a set of seventy-four plates showing a variety of picturesque or down at heel streetsellers, spiced with

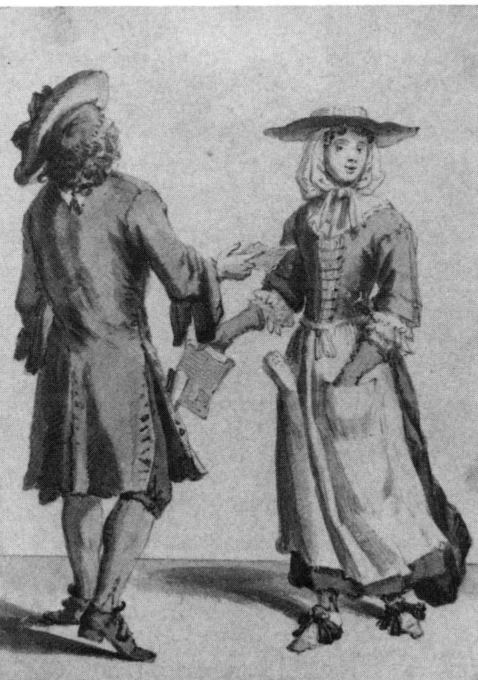

31

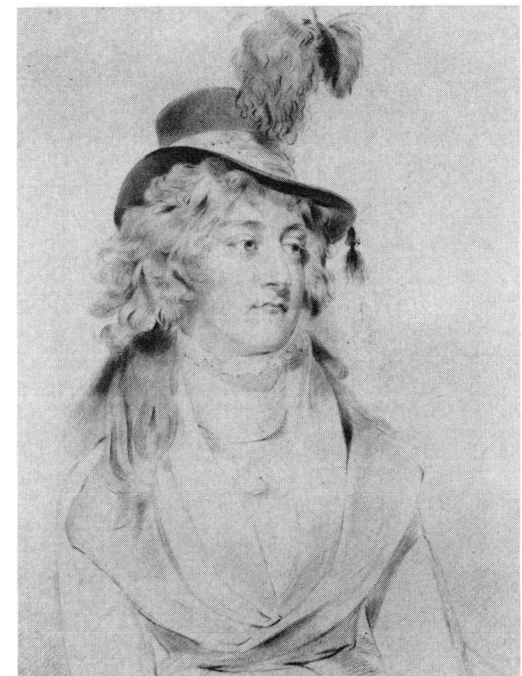

33

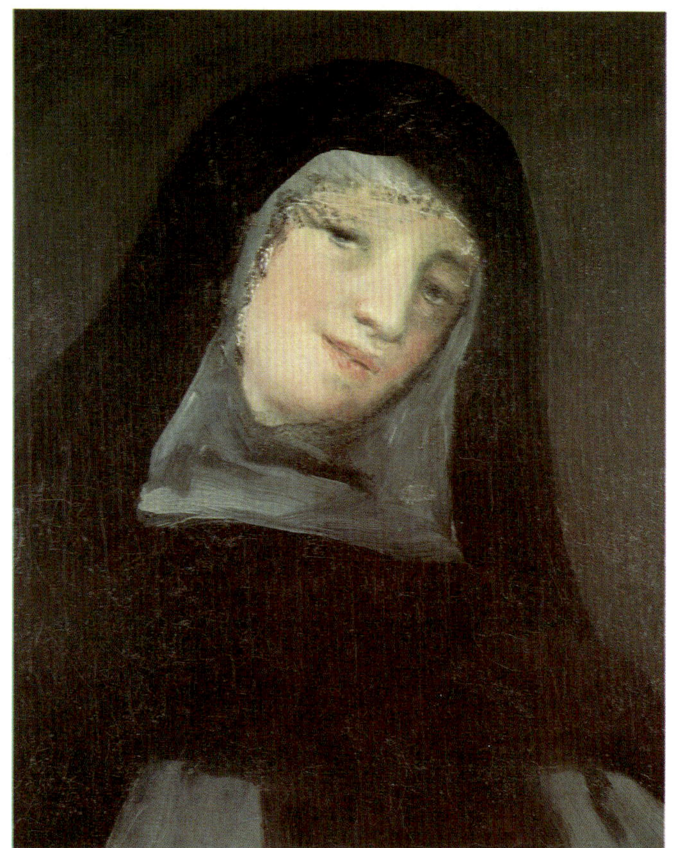

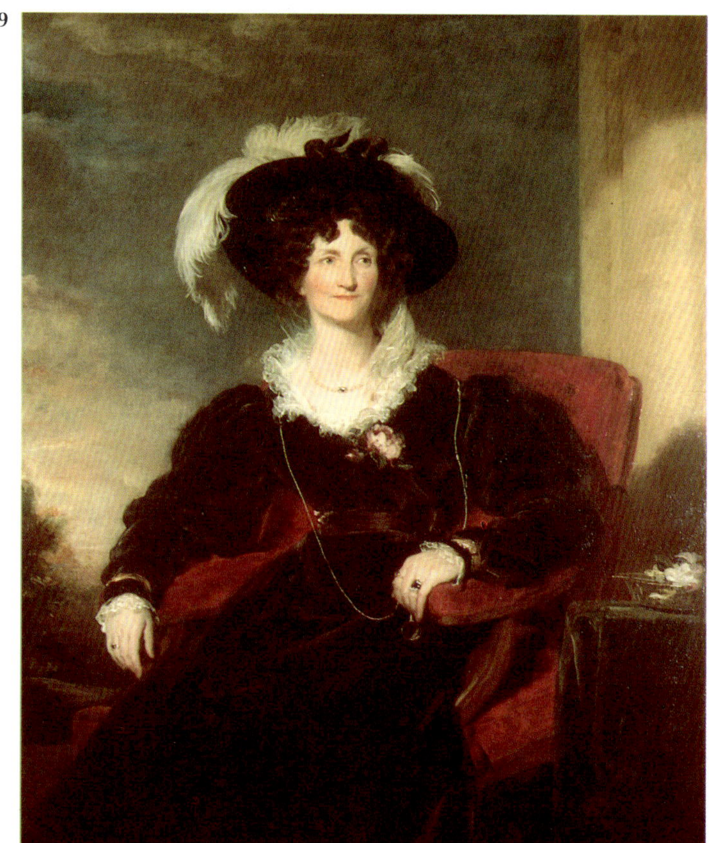

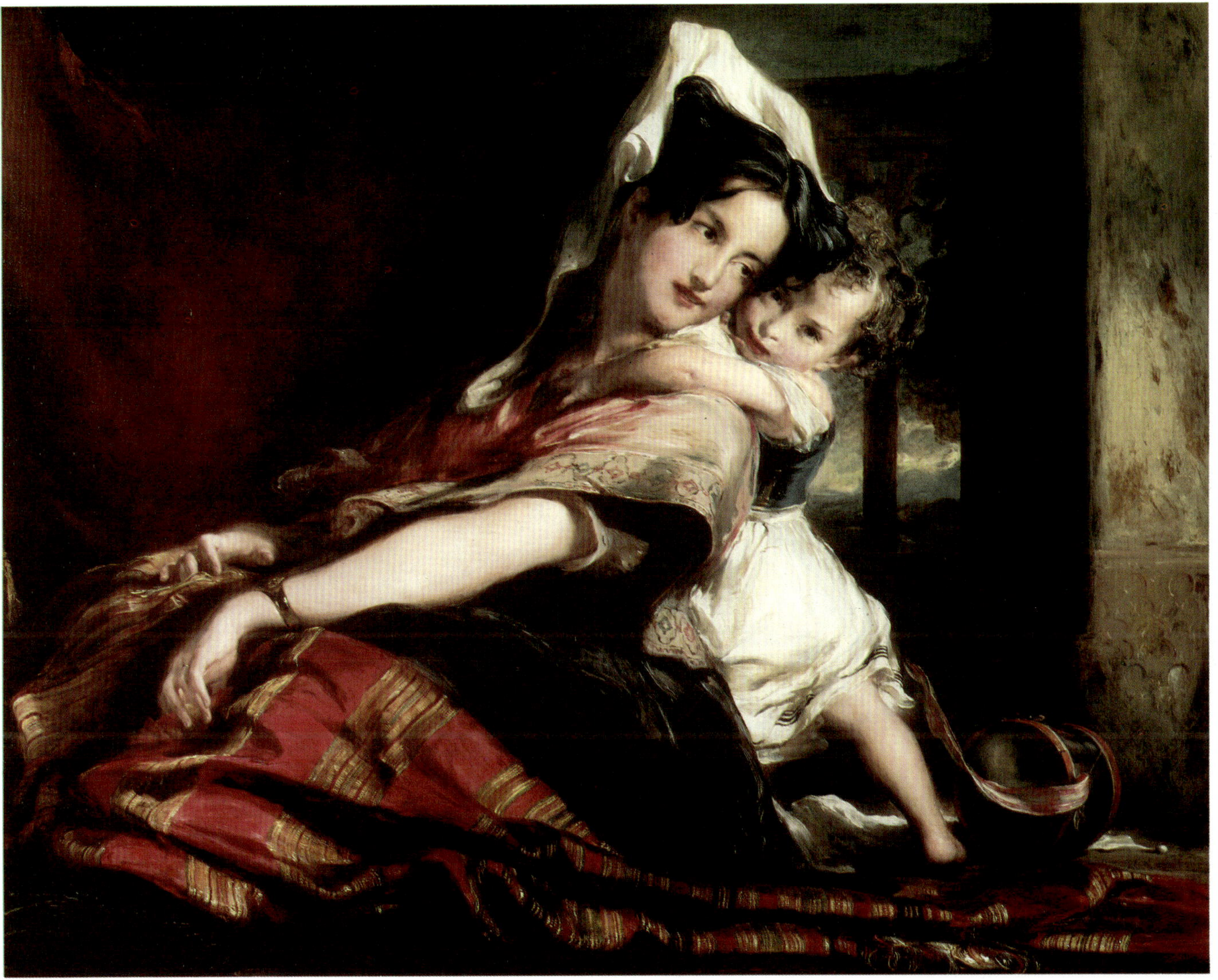

humour, was first announced in 1687. Published by Pierce Tempest with a European market in mind, the series was probably inspired by J. Bonnart's *Cris de Paris* of *c.* 1676, while an important earlier example of the genre is the *Arti di Bologna* after drawings by Annibale Carracci.

Lit.: S. Shesgreen, *The Criers and Hawkers of London, Engravings and Drawings by Marcellus Laroon* (Aldershot, 1990).

32 Sir Thomas Lawrence (1769–1830) *Mrs Benjamin Gott*
Oil on canvas. 142.2 : 111.8

Mrs Gott (née Elizabeth Rhodes) was the wife of a wealthy factory owner. Benjamin Gott, of Armley House, Leeds, was a friend of John Flaxman and Francis Chantrey and an important patron of the arts in Leeds. This portrait was painted in 1827 with its companion of *Mr Benjamin Gott*. Lawrence conducted a fascinating correspondance with Mrs Gott as to the lighting, hanging and framing of the pictures which he considered to be 'two of the best I ever painted'.

Lit.: K. Garlick, *Sir Thomas Lawrence* (Oxford, 1989), no.341.

33 Sir Thomas Lawrence (1769–1830) *Elizabeth Lysons*
Pencil drawing. 24.2 : 18

Lawrence painted other members of the family, notably Samuel Lysons, the antiquary, and the Revd. Daniel Lysons, but the sitter's relationship to them is not known. There is a version of this portrait at Yale, dated 1795, which is identical. Lawrence replicated a drawing with extraordinary precision on several occasions.

34 Frederick, Lord Leighton (1830–1896) *The Staircase of a House at Capri*
Oil on canvas. 27.2 : 30

Leighton spent five weeks in Capri in the spring of 1859. This is typical of the small open-air sketches of courtyards, passages and

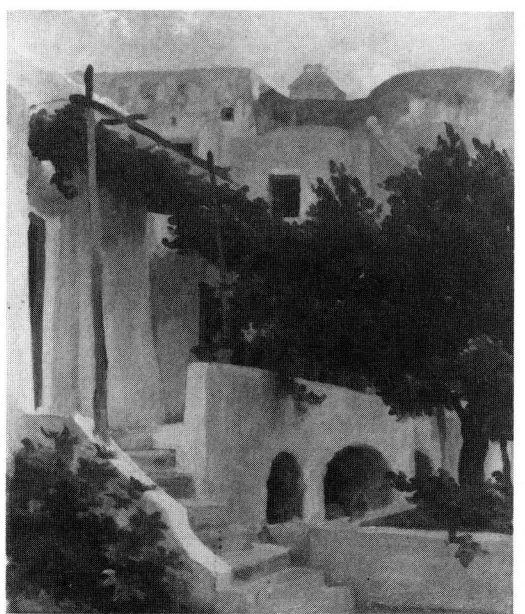

34

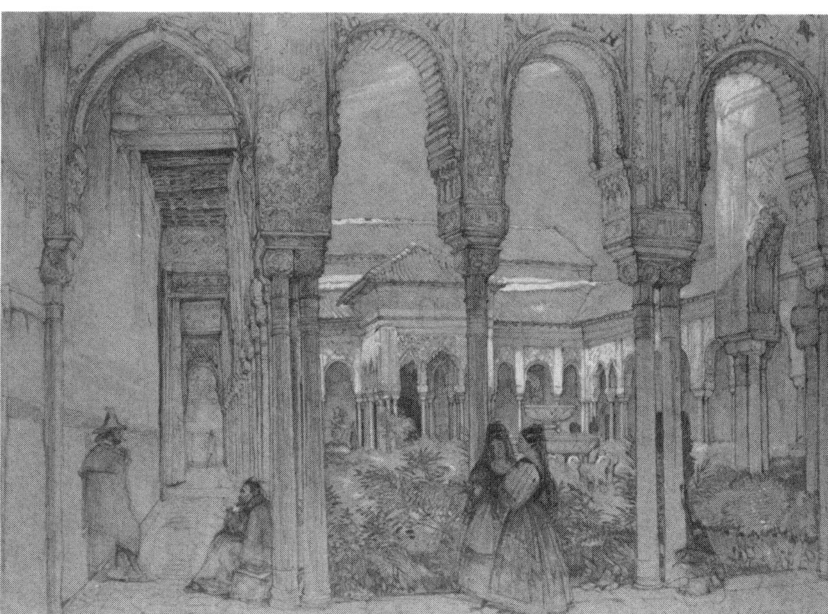

35

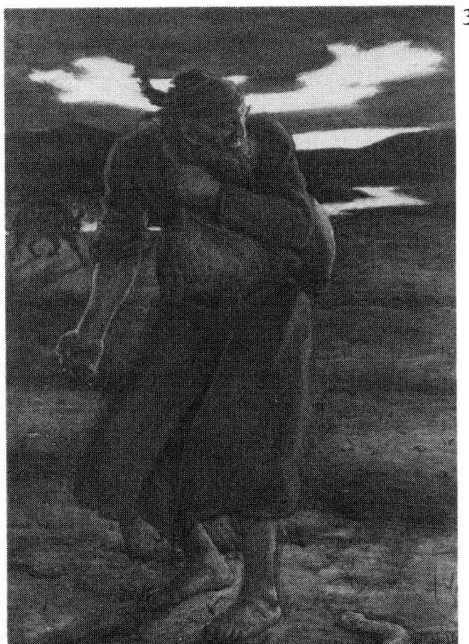

37

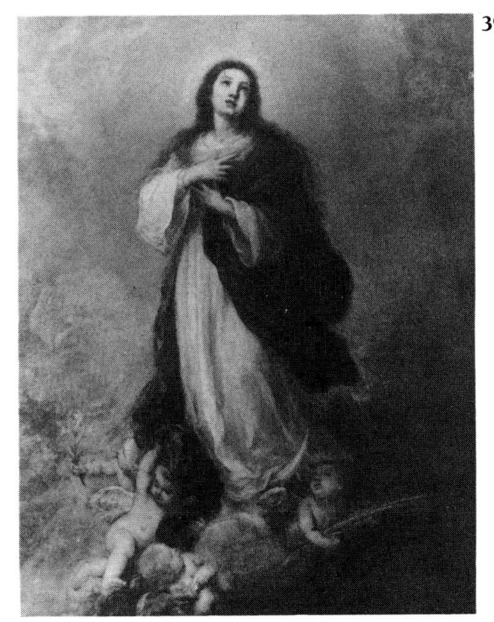

39

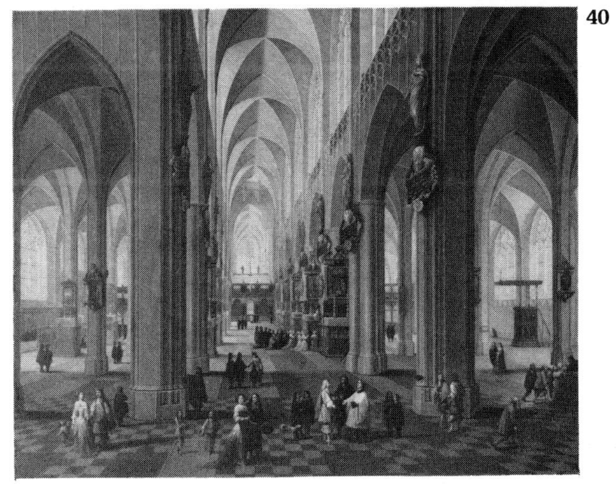

40

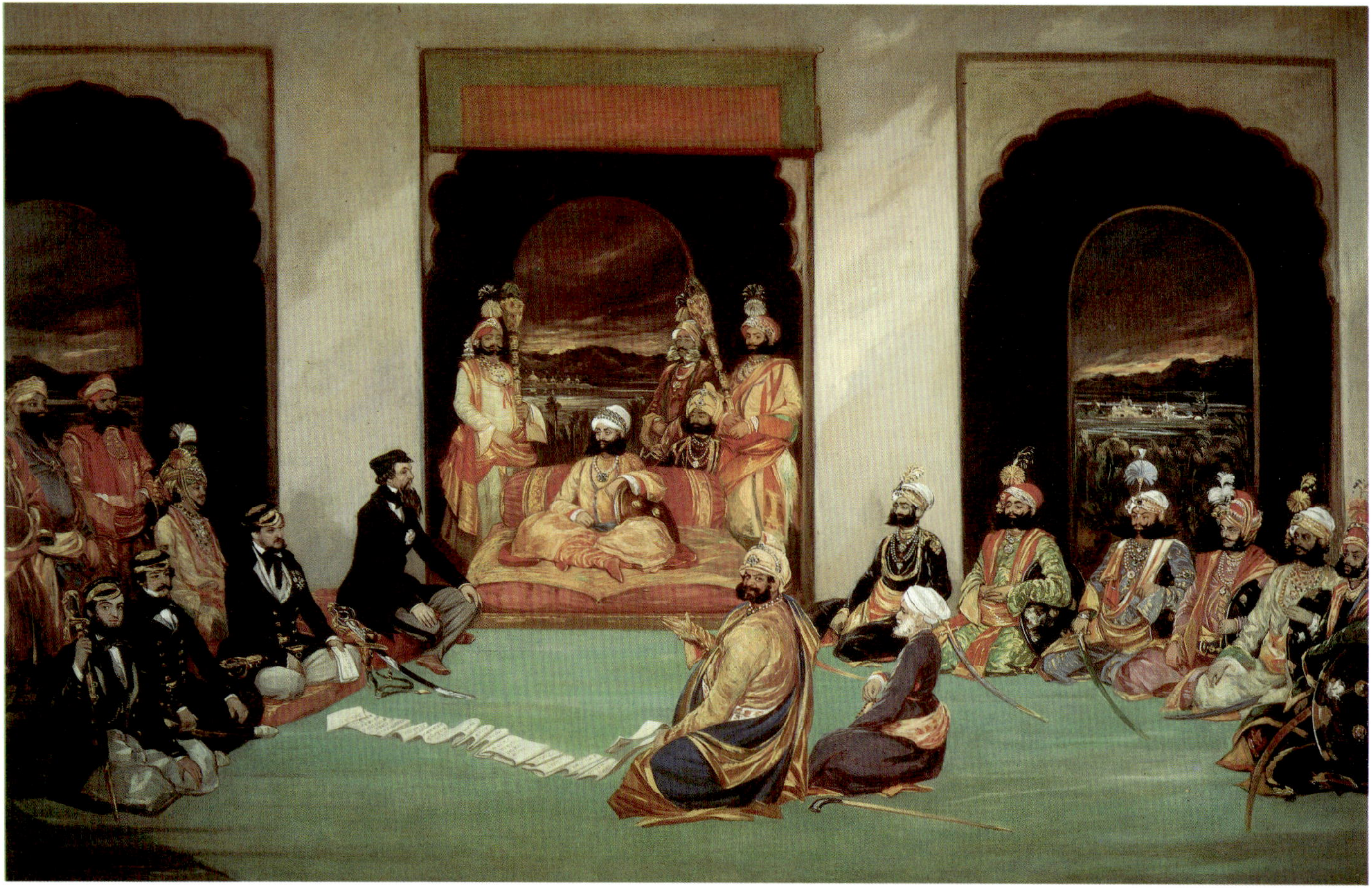

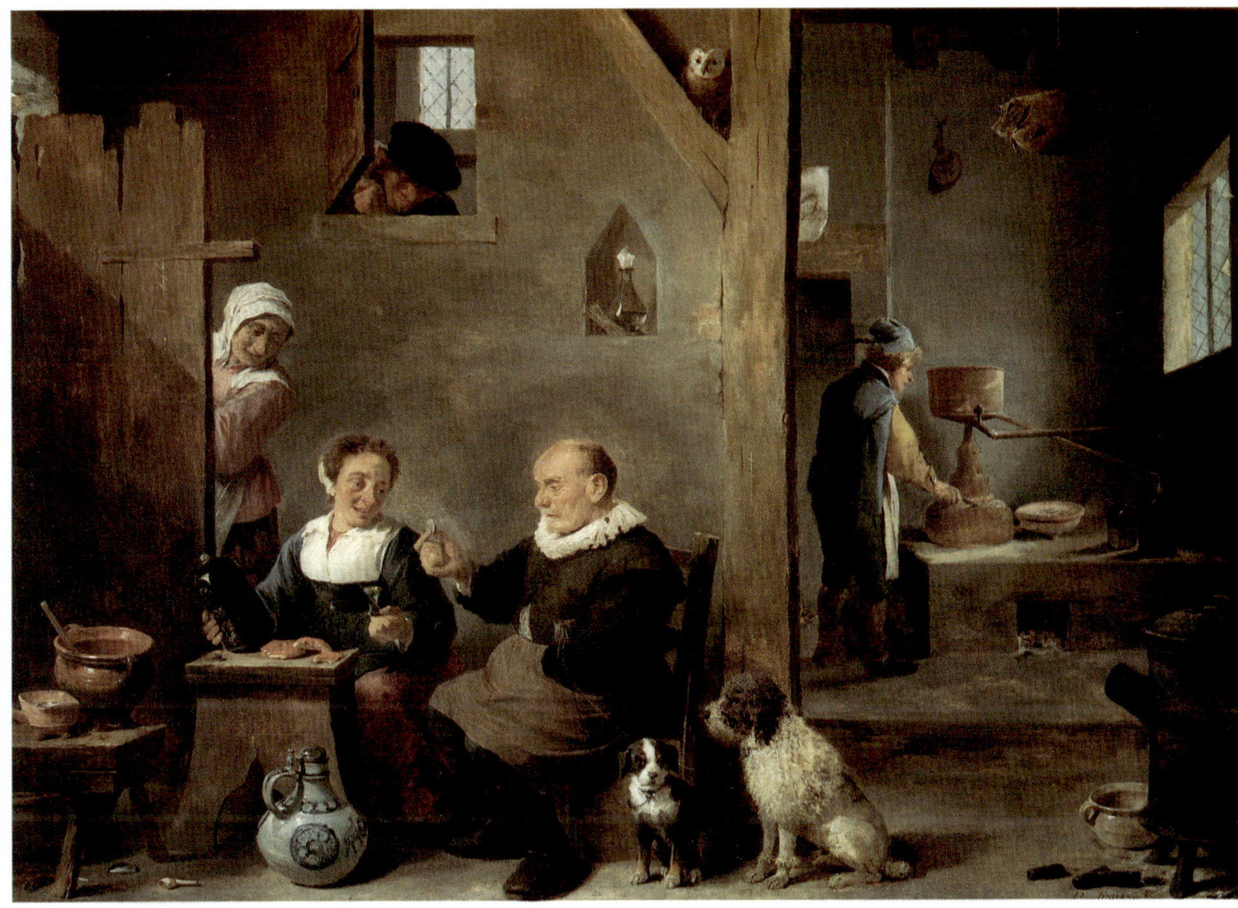

streets that he painted there, invariably juxtaposing white architecture with trees and greenery, and sunlit areas with those in shadow.
Lit.: Catalogue, *The Loyd Collection* (1991), no.41.

35 John Frederick Lewis (1805–1876) *View of the Alhambra at Granada*
Pencil, watercolour and bodycolour on grey paper. 30.6 : 20.6 (sight). Inscribed lower right: *Patio de los Leones*

This was reproduced as plate 20 in the second of two volumes of lithographs, *Lewis's Sketches of Spain and Spanish Character, made during his Tour in that Country, in 1833–34* London, 1836. This volume was dedicated to Lewis's forerunner in Spain, Sir David Wilkie (see no.69). This period in Spain finally established Lewis as an important artist. His colour became so exuberant that, on viewing the Spanish drawings, J.S. Cotman wrote, 'Words cannot convey to you their splendour'.

36 Frederick Christian Lewis (1813–1875) *The Darbar at Udaipur*
Oil on canvas. 11.6 : 27.1. An inscription held by the main British protagonist reads: *Col. G. St. P. Lawrence/Dalhousie/ Megawar (?)*

A much travelled artist who moved further east than his brother John Frederick, Lewis found a ready market in the princely courts of India for his confident portraits. He made a speciality during his three sojourns in India of portraits of glittering rulers surrounded by courtiers, often with members of the British Residency: some of these were engraved by his father F.C. Lewis and his brother Charles. This appears to be a version of the painting in the India

42

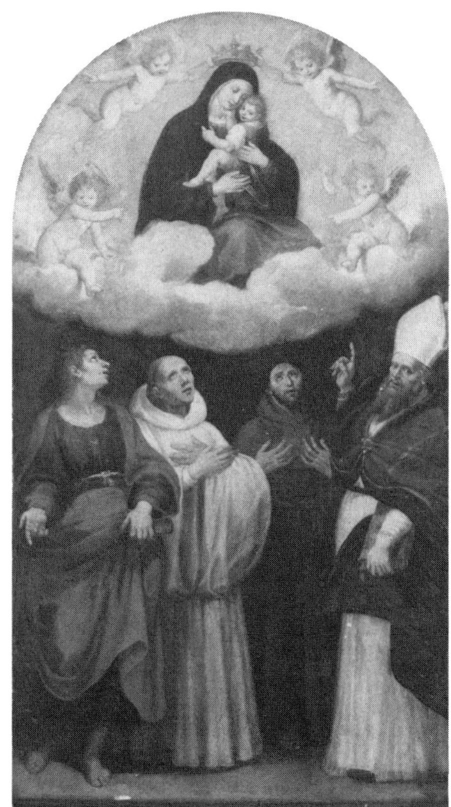

41

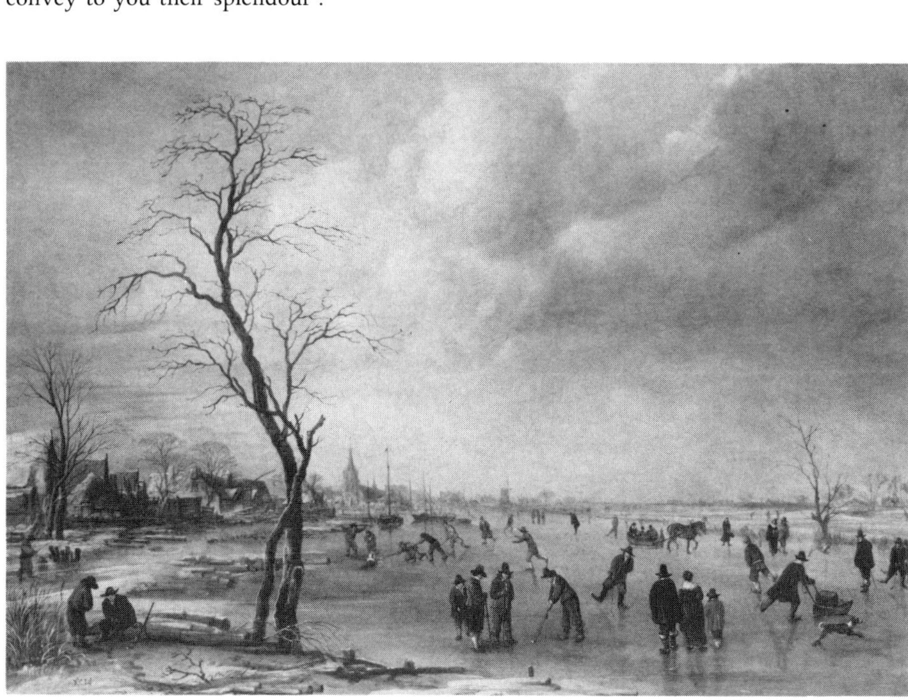

Office Library showing the darbar (or levée) at Udaipur, Rajasthan, held in February 1855 to sign a treaty – unfolded in the foreground – between the Maharana of Udaipur and his Sardars or chiefs and the British. There are a number of variations in no.36, particularly in the background and figures standing on the right.

Lit.: See M. Archer, *The India Office Collection of Paintings and Sculpture* (London, 1986), no.73.

37 Sir John Everett Millais Bt. PRA (1829–1896) *The Enemy sewing Tares*

Watercolour and bodycolour on paper. 24.5 : 17 (sight)

In 1863 the Dalziel brothers published a book of the Parables with twenty illustrations by Millais. The designs for these were reused by the artist in a number of variants of the mid 1860s. *The Enemy sewing Tares* (Matt.13.24) reappears in a watercolour (Whitworth,

Manchester) and in a larger oil (Birmingham Art Gallery). This fourth version follows the others closely. The scene is set at night, in keeping with the text, but the wolf and snake, attributes of the Evil One, are not mentioned in the Parable.

38 Sir Alfred Munnings RA (1878–1959) *Fancy Dress Party: the Chelsea Arts Club*

Oil on canvas. 49 : 29.5. Signed: *AJ Munnings 01*

Despite losing the sight of his right eye in 1899, Munnings went on to become a highly successful painter. This early work, with its vivid, strong colours and rich impasto, is delightfully spirited. The Chelsea Arts Club was founded in 1891 for social intercourse between practitioners of both the plastic and graphic arts. Annual fancy dress parties were held in the studios from 1887 and later on in Chelsea Town Hall, which is probably the location here: the first

43

44

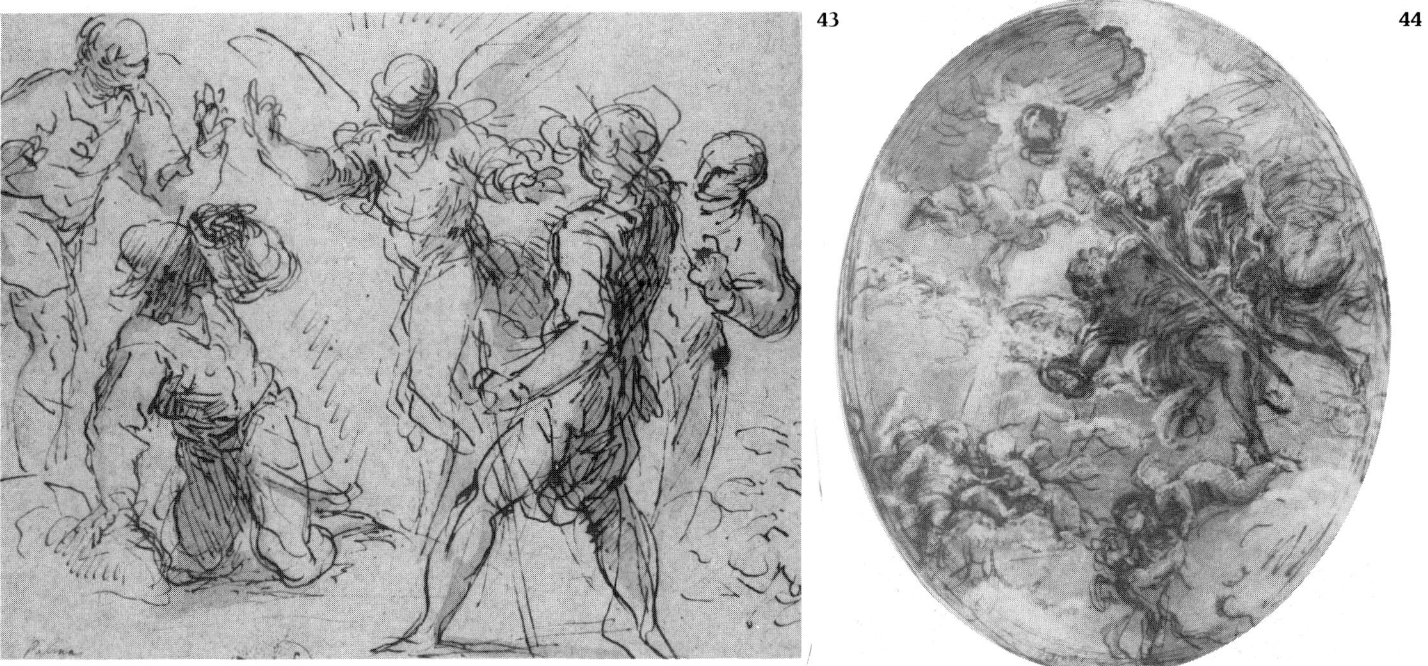

of the formal balls was not until 1908. Munnings was expelled from the Club in 1920 for bad behaviour, but his popularity was such that there was a movement to reinstate him and he was later re-elected.

39 Bartolome Esteban Murillo (1617/18–1682) *The Immaculate Conception*
Oil on canvas. 36 : 27.3
This is Murillo's *modello* for the picture now in the Detroit Institute of Arts, painted *c.*1670 by his workshop with some minor variations. The Immaculate Conception was an extremely popular subject in Spanish seventeenth century art. Fervour for the cult grew after a pontifical brief in its favour in 1661. Murillo encapsulated this complex set of beliefs into a powerful visual image.
　　Lit.: Catalogue, *The Loyd Collection* (1991), no.47.

40 Peter Neefs the Elder (c.1578–1656/61) *Interior of Antwerp Cathedral*
Oil on canvas. 69 : 84.5. Signed and dated: *PEETER/NEEFS/D.A./1653*
The artist's *oeuvre* largely consists of variations of the interior of Antwerp Cathedral, often including imaginary paintings and sculptural detail. The figures, usually painted by other hands, are reputed to be by Gonzales Coques.

41 Aert van der Neer (1603/4–1677) *Skaters and Kolf Players on the Ice*
Oil on panel. 49 : 67.5. Signed with the monogram: *AVDN.*
Van der Neer worked as an innkeeper as well as a painter, ending his life in considerable poverty. This is a characteristic winter scene by the artist, set before an imaginary town or village and successfully suggesting the scale of the Dutch landscape. *Kolf* was played in winter on the ice with a curved stick as in hockey today.

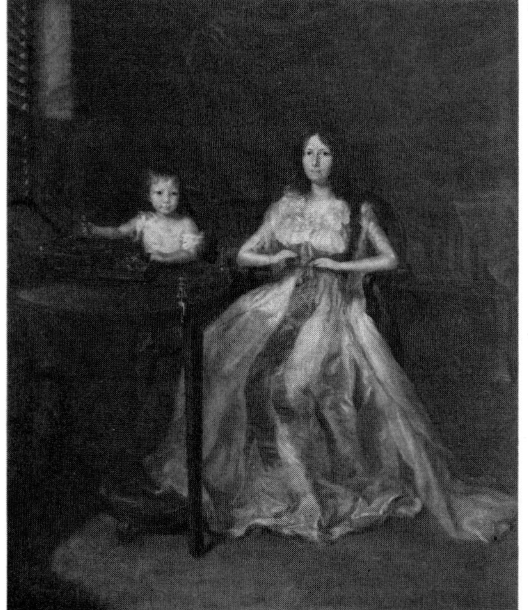

45

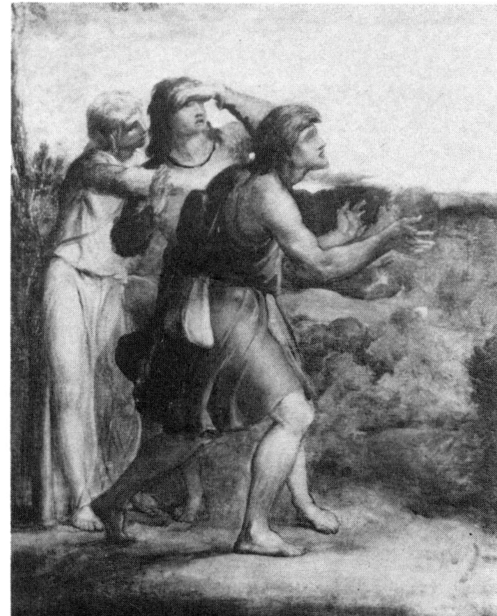

46

42 Avanzino Nucci (?1551–1629) *Madonna and Child with Saints John the Evangelist, Bruno, Francis and a Bishop Saint*
Oil on panel. 51 : 27

Possibly a private devotional picture of the 1570s, this was recognized by H. Röttgen as a work by the little-known Avanzino Nucci on the basis of its connection with a drawing in the Walker Art Gallery, Liverpool (no.5083). Philip Pouncey, who originally identified the hand of Nucci in a group of some fifty drawings, agreed.

43 Jacopo Palma il Giovane (*c.*1548–1628) *The Angel Appearing to the Shepherds*
Pen and ink and brown wash on buff paper. 15.6 : 19.8. Inscribed: *Palma*

Palma Giovane was a most prolific draughtsman, who made drawings for prints and book illustrations and as independent works, as well as in preparation for paintings. The dating of his drawings is difficult, but this seems to be a mature work, where the rapidly sketched penstrokes and the judicious use of wash effectively convey the drama of the scene and the burst of light around the angel.

Lit.: *Pleasure in Drawings* (Barnard Castle, Bowes Museum, and Newcastle, Hatton Gallery, 1980), no.3.

44 Giuseppe Passeri (1654–1714) *Study for St. Joseph in Glory*
Pen and dark brown ink and wash heightened with white on paper washed brown Oval 29.1 : 24.1. Inscribed on the drawing: *Passeri* and on the mount: *da Passeri*

A preparatory drawing for Passeri's fresco in the cupola of the chapel of S. Giuseppe (built in 1686) in the church of S. Francesco a Ripa, Rome. St Joseph carries his attribute of a flowering rod. This is a characteristic work, highly elaborate and painterly because it comes at a very late stage in the preparatory process.

Lit.: Exhibition catalogue, *Pleasure in Drawings* (Barnard Castle, Bowes Museum, and Newcastle, Hatton Galley, 1980), no.10.

45 Francesco Renaldi (1755–post 1798) *Portrait of Mrs William Douglas (1769–1795) and her Son Philip (1786–1867)*
Oil on canvas. 106 : 90. Previously recorded as signed; no longer visible.

The sitter was the daughter of Major John Bell of Rhode Island. In 1785 she married in Calcutta Judge William Douglas (1755–1802), who was 3rd Judge of the Court of Appeal at Moorshedabad. The picture was probably painted in 1789/80 when their son Philip

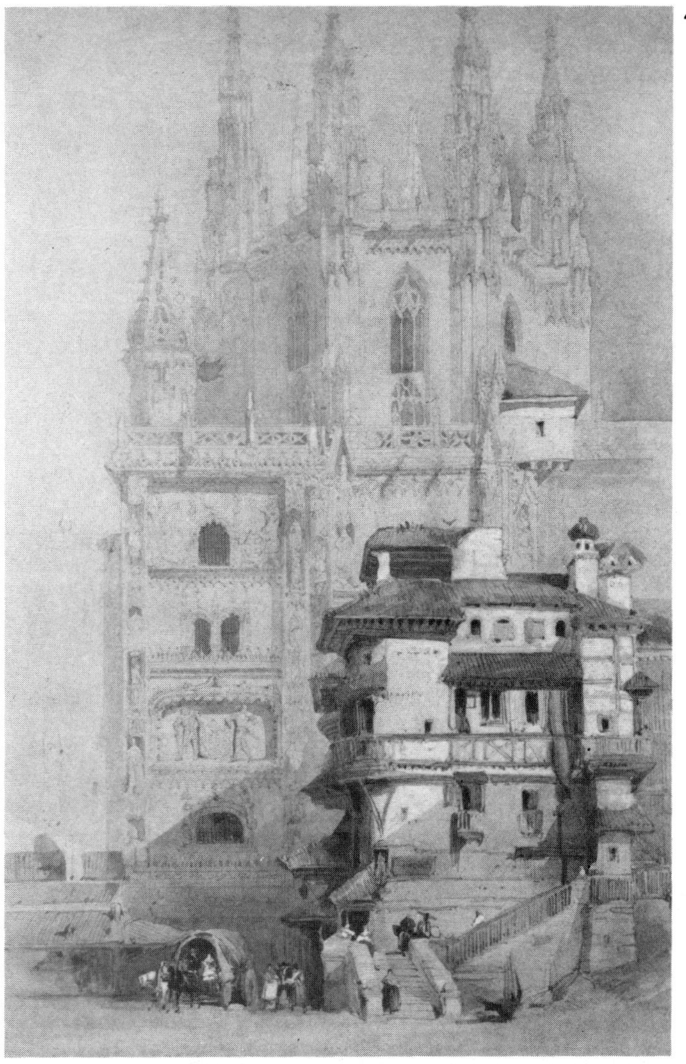

Henry was aged about three. Despite his Italian parentage, Renaldi was born and trained in England. He settled in India from 1786–1796, painting portraits of European families resident there. Few have survived: this one remains in the family of the descendants.

Lit.: *A History of the Douglas Family of Morton in Nithsdale (Dumfriesshire) and Fingland (Kircudbrightshire) and their Descendants* (Bedford, 1921).

46 George Richmond RA (1809–1896) *Christian on the Delectable Mountain from 'Pilgrim's Progress'.*
Oil sketch on canvas. 47.5 : 37.5
The scene is thought to be in the Delectable Mountains, towards the end of *Pilgrim's Progress* when Christian (right) and Hopeful (centre) are being shown the Shining Gates of the Heavenly City by Knowledge. The Richmond family, who owned this sketch, believed that Christian was modelled on the artist's close friend Samuel Palmer. They first met in the circle of the elderly William Blake. Like the other two painters, Richmond had a preference for subjects that were both literary and visionary. A drawing of Palmer relating to this sketch was formerly in the Richmond collection.

47 David Roberts (1796–1864) *The Chapter House, Burgos Cathedral*
Pencil, brown wash and watercolour. 41.5 : 26.5 (sight)
Roberts visited Spain in 1832–3: the many sketches he made were the basis for more elaborate views produced in England. He was fascinated by the Moorish elements in southern Spanish architecture and culture. This view of *c.*1836 was reproduced in a lithograph by T.S. Boys as plate VII of the *Picturesque Sketches in Spain* (1837).

Lit.: H. Guiterman and B. Llewellyn, *David Roberts* (Barbican Art Gallery, London, 1986), no.84.

48 Dante Gabriel Rossetti (1822–1882) *Portrait of Christina Rossetti (1830–1894)*
Oil on canvas. 16 : 15 (sight). Inscribed and dated: *C.G.R. by D.G.R. 1848*
William Michael Rossetti described this compelling portrait as the

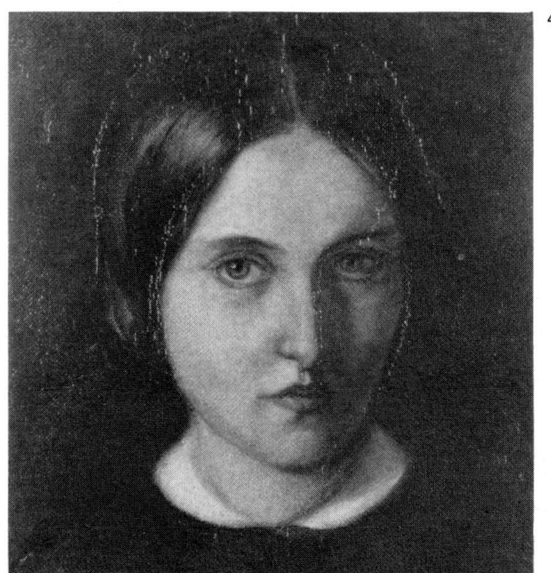

48

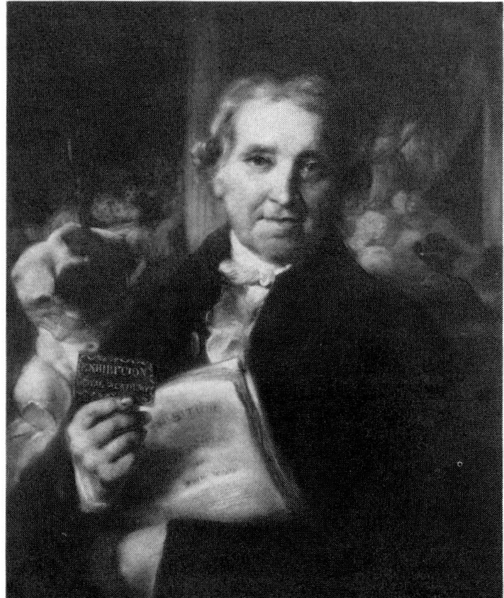

49

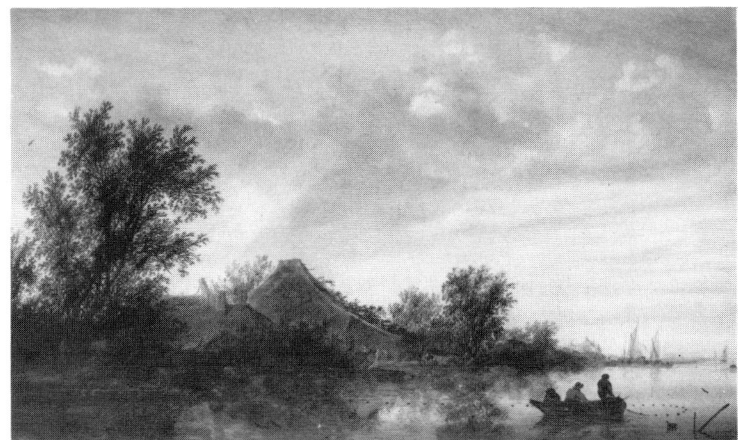
50

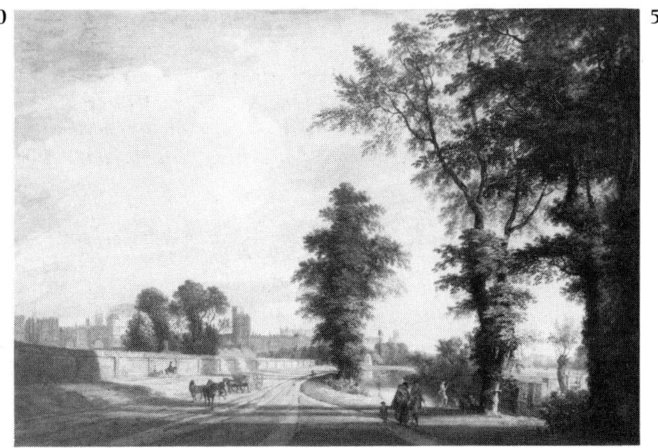
51

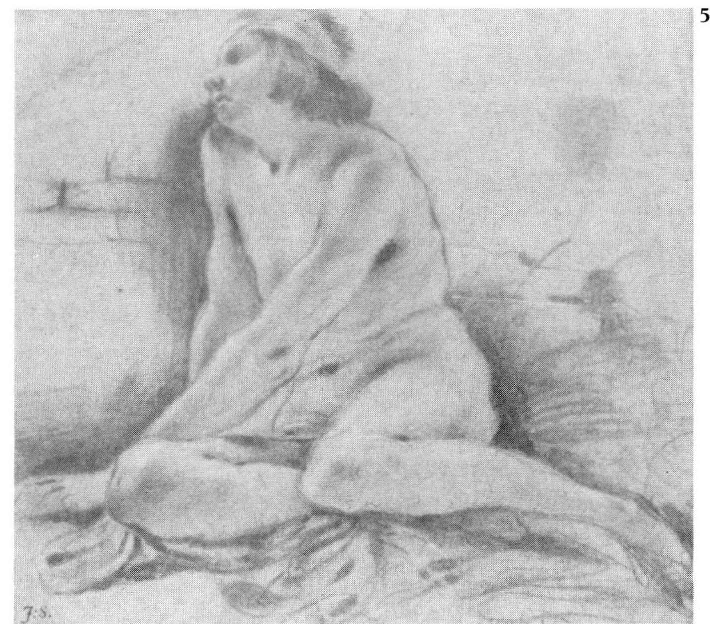
52

first oil painting finished by his brother. A precocious poetess, Christina had already had two small volumes of verses composed by this date. Her poetry is invariably melancholic, expressing the agonies of disappointed love. A devout high Anglican, she spent much time caring for her family and in charitable works.

Lit.: Exhibition catalogue, *Dante Gabriel Rossetti, painter and poet* (Royal Academy, London, 1973).

49 John Russell (1745-1806) *The Porter at the Royal Academy*
Pastel. 72.3 : 59 (sight)
A pupil of Francis Cotes, Russell was, like his master, a great admirer of the technique and rich colouring of the pastels of Rosalba Carriera. Here, he obtains a striking softness of effect and luminosity through the careful rubbing or smudging of his pastel crayons.

50 Salomon van Ruysdael (c.1600–1670) *River Scene with a Ferry*
Oil on panel. 51.5 : 82. Signed and dated: *SvR 1644*
On the left, a ferry boat with cattle and on the right a rowing boat with three men fishing. The painting, with its feeling for atmosphere, is typical of his river scenes, which usually recede diagonally into the distance.

Lit.: W. Stechow, *Salomon van Ruysdael* (Berlin, 1938), no.342.

51 Paul Sandby (1730/1–1809) *Windsor Castle from Datchet Lane*
Watercolour and bodycolour. 38 : 54.5
Sandby made a great number of views of Windsor in the 1760s and 1770s, including some from Datchet Lane (now Road) which runs beneath the north wall of the castle. Here he has chosen a low viewpoint, with a large expanse of beautifully-lit sky, and picturesque foliage. This view is very close to a pencil and watercolour drawing in the Royal Collection, which in turn is based on the etching of the same subject in the small series of Windsor views of 1780.

Lit.: see P. Oppé, *The Drawings of Paul and Thomas Sandby in the collection of His Majesty the King at Windsor Castle* (London, 1947), no.69.

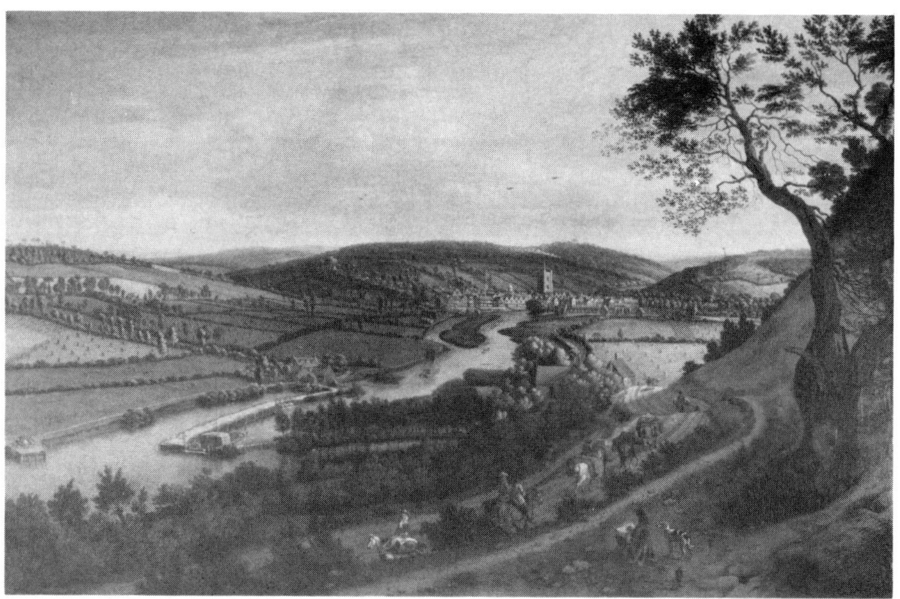

53

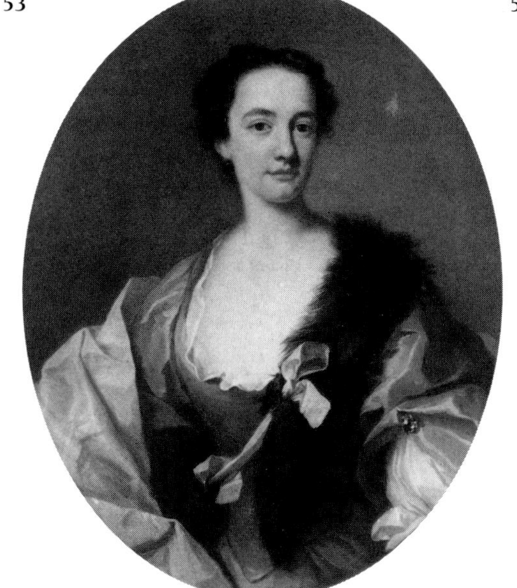

54

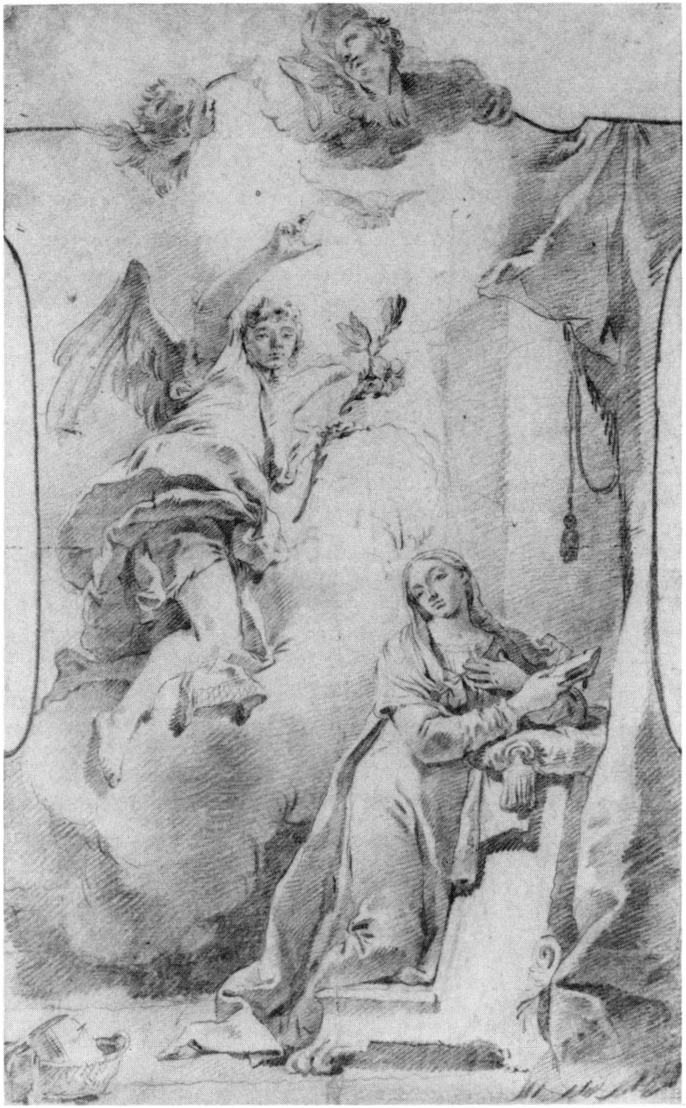

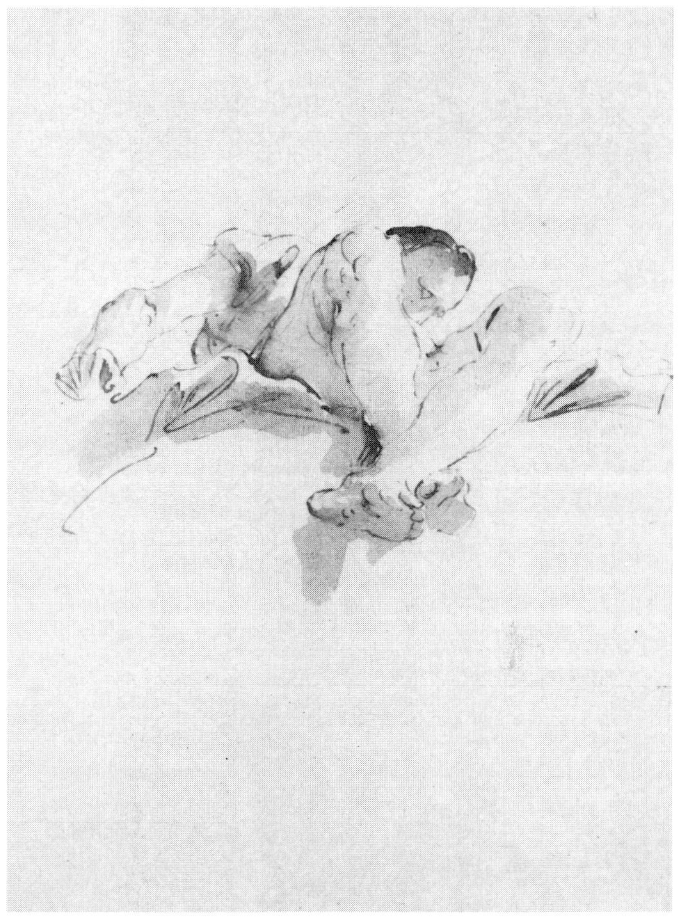

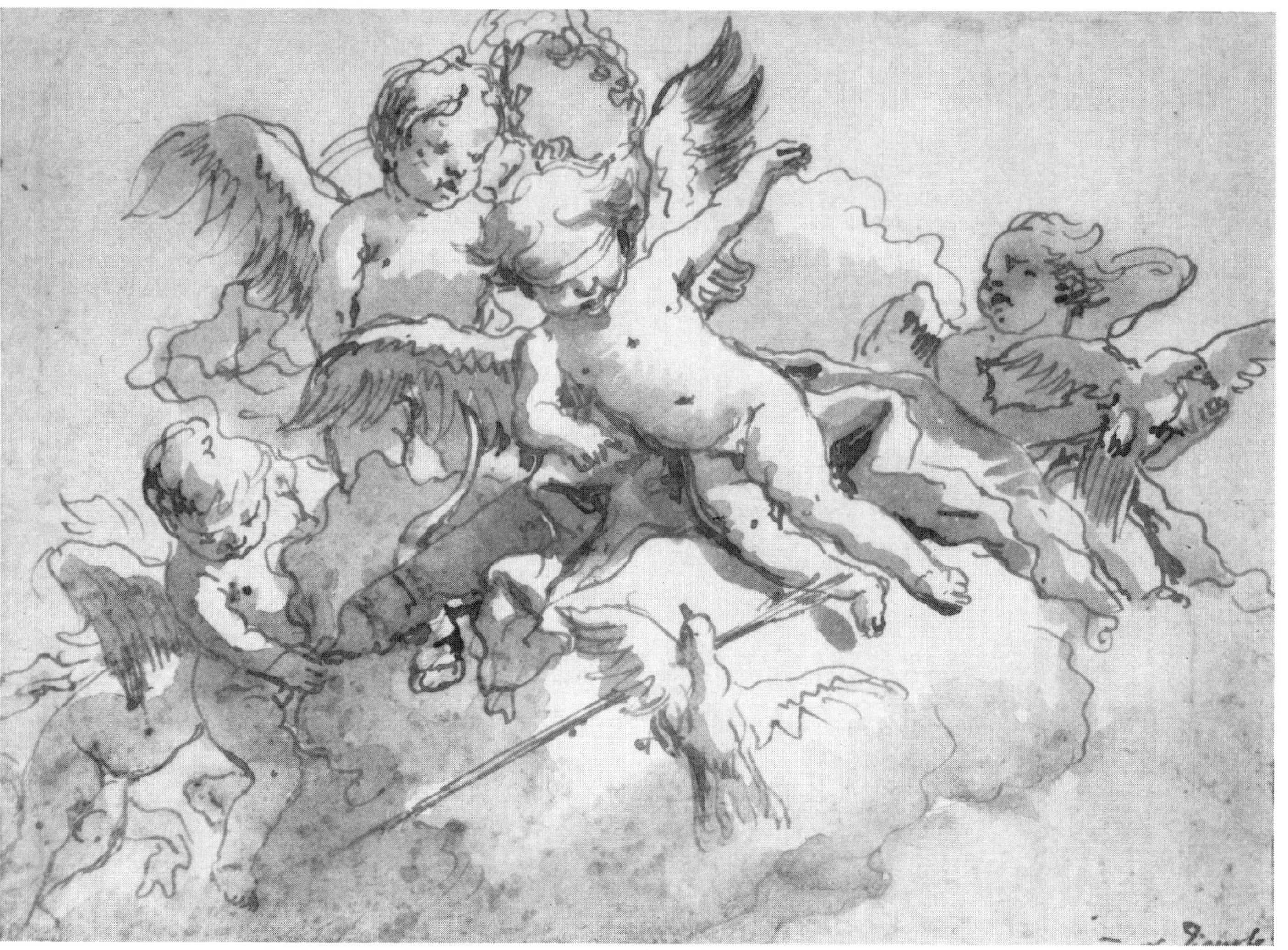

52 Ascribed to Bartolommeo Schedoni (1578–1615) *Nude Figure*
Red chalk with a little wash on buff paper. 17.6 : 18.5
This study was probably made from the life, with emphasis on light and shade. Indications of a brick wall behind and some straw on the right have been added, suggesting that the artist was visualising the figure in an outdoor setting, perhaps with a narrative painting in mind. A polished effect is achieved by the combination of red chalk and wash, a favourite technique of Schedoni, to whom the drawing was attributed by an early owner, the collector John Skippe (1742–1812). However the idiosyncratic treatment of the form (as in the long, tapering limbs, or the quirky line of the hip) is unlike Schedoni. The drawing is possibly by an Emilian contemporary.

53 Jan Siberechts (1627–1703) *View of Henley from the Wargrave Road*
Oil on canvas. 83 : 126.5. Signed and dated: *J. Siberechts 16.*
Siberechts, a landscape painter from Antwerp, arrived in England in 1672 or shortly afterwards. As well as executing views of country houses, he painted English scenery. An artist is sketching in the foreground, before a panorama which includes Marsh Lock and its toll bridge, and the tower of St, Mary's church dominating the town. Siberechts painted several different views of the town.
Lit.: T-H Fokker, *Jan Siberechts, Peintre de la Paysage Flamand* (Brussels, 1931), pl.42.

54 Andrea Soldi (*c.*1703–1771) *Portrait of a Lady*
Oil on canvas. Oval 74.5 : 60.5 (sight)
Soldi, born in Florence, painted portraits of British merchants in Constantinople and Aleppo, which probably led him to try his fortune in London from 1736. The painting dates from *c.*1740. He enjoyed much success up to the mid-1740s with his elegant style, attractive colour and occasional exotic details. Soldi's fortunes declined with the rise of Reynolds and Ramsay: he could not compete with portraits in the grand manner, nor with the growing taste for sober characterization.

55 David Teniers (1610–1690) *The Apothecary's Shop*
Oil on panel;. 46.8 : 64 (sight). Signed: *D. Teniers F*
The artist was a keen satirist of human behaviour. The quackery implicit in the transaction between the woman and the old man, who clutches his medicine, is emphasised by the inclusion of an owl, normally in the Netherlands associated with folly.

56 Giovanni Battista Tiepolo (1696–1770) *The Annunciation*
Black chalk. 28.8 : 17.6
This carefully executed composition with its decoratively shaped border was possibly intended for the engraver, to be published as a devotional image or a book illustration. An early work, this drawing shows Tiepolo's strong interest in the art of Piazzetta. The subject was a favourite one with Tiepolo.
Lit.: Exhibition catalogue, *Eighteenth Century Venice* (Whitechapel Gallery, London, 1951), no.126.

57 Giovanni Battista Tiepolo (1696–1770) *Seated Figure*
Pen and brown ink and wash. 18.3 : 13.3
One of a large group of more than 170 drawings which were originally bound up in an album entitled *Sole figure per soffitti* (single figures for ceilings), this rapidly drawn foreshortened figure could have been made for its own sake or with a small detail of a fresco in mind, probably in the late 1750s.
Lit.: *Art Vénitien en Suisse et au Lichtenstein* (Musée d'art et d'histoire, Geneva, 1978), no.127.

58 Giovanni Domenico Tiepolo (1727–1804) *Cupid and Putti at Play*
Pen and ink and brown wash. 18.1 : 24.4. Signed
Domenico explored a number of favourite subjects in independent pen and ink drawings, producing several variations on a theme. This is one of a group of compositions with blindfold cupids and *amoretti* playing about in the clouds: Domenico's inspiration for this subject may have been the frescoes at the Foresteria in the Villa Valmarana, where he worked with his father Giambattista in 1757.
Lit.: *Pleasure in Drawings* (Barnard Castle, Bowes Museum, and Newcastle, Hatton Gallery, 1980), no.15.

59 Francesco Trevisani (1656–1746) *The Penitent Magdalen*
Oil on canvas. 64.5 : 48.2
A Venetian artist who made his career in Rome, Trevisani was very popular with Grand Tourists. This is similar to a picture in the Clerk Collection at Penicuik, painted in Rome in 1739 and bought by James Clerk. The apocryphal subject of the penitent Mary Magdalen, who lived a life of prayer and asceticism after the Resurrection, was an extremely popular one with collectors, as it combined a serious moral message with an attractive image.

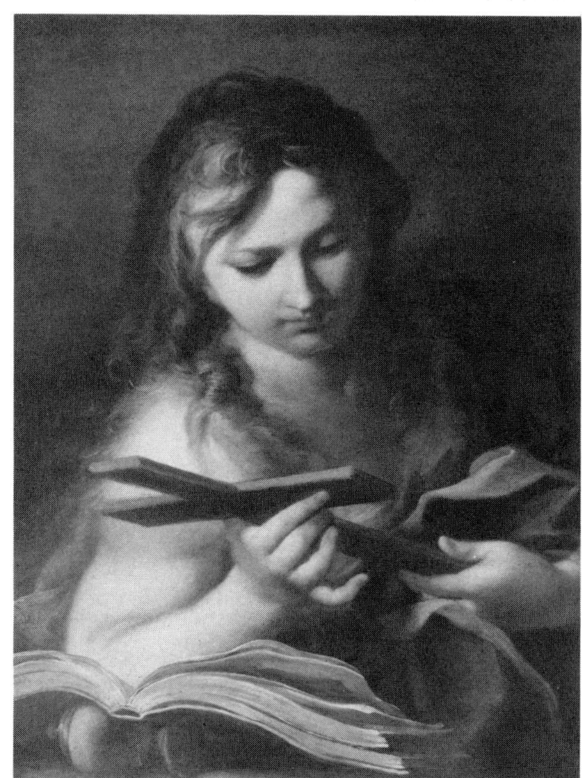

59

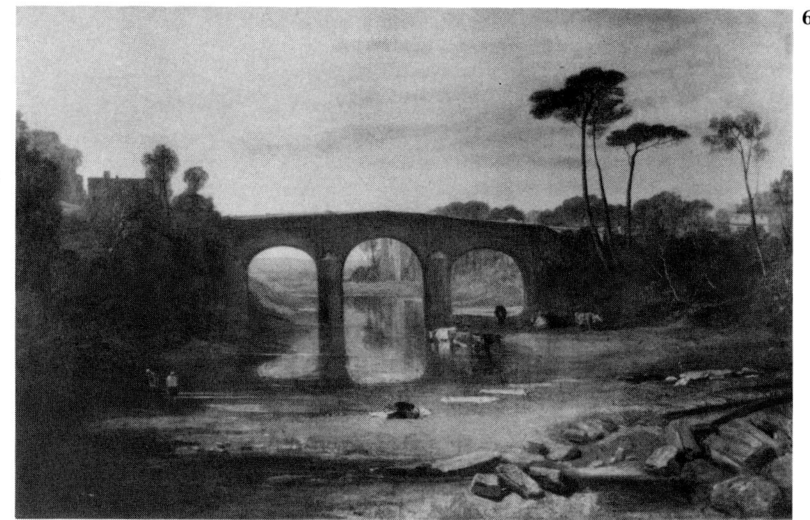

61

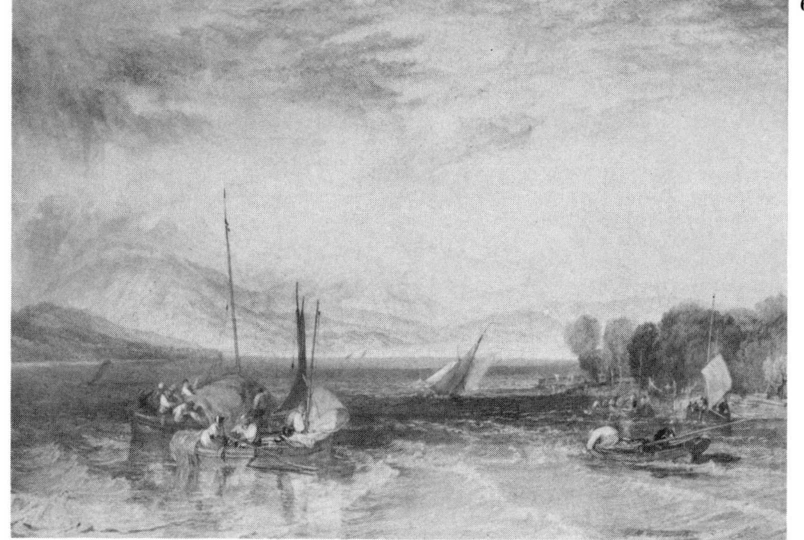

62

60 Joseph Mallord William Turner (1775–1851) *View of the High Street, Oxford*

Oil on canvas. 68.5 : 99.5. Signed: *J M W Turner* RA

A related drawing in the Turner Bequest at the Tate Gallery shows the scene from a slightly different viewpoint. The picture was commissioned by the Oxford picture dealer and frame-maker James Wyatt (1774–1853), for use as the basis of an engraving that he wished to publish. Following a first drawing in December 1809, Turner completed the picture and sent it to Oxford in April 1810. It was exhibited back in London the next month, at Turner's Gallery in Harley Street, and at the Royal Academy in 1812. Turner agreed to Wyatt's request for changes. Wyatt was very pleased with the picture and commissioned a companion one, *View of Oxford from the Abingdon Road* (Private Collection).

> Lit.: Catalogue, *The Loyd Collection* (1991), no.61.

61 Joseph Mallord William Turner (1775–1851) *Whalley Bridge and Abbey, Lancashire*

Oil on canvas. 61.2: 92.3

Turner made a drawing of this scene in the summer of 1808, while visiting Sir John Leicester's seat, Tabley House, near Knutsford, Cheshire. The painting may have been commissioned by Thomas Lister Parker of Browsholme, and shows both the influence of Claude and the naturalism so evident in Turner's work at this time.

> Lit.: Catalogue, *The Loyd Collection* (1991), no.62.

62 Joseph Mallord William Turner (1775–1851) *Windermere*

Watercolour. Signed and dated lower right *J. M. W. Turner 1821*

First owned by Turner's friend and patron Walter Fawkes of Farnley Hall, Yorkshire, the watercolour is one of a group of five Lake District views commissioned by Fawkes. The sketchbooks from which Turner worked these up include drawings of the Farnley estate as well of Fawkes' other house, Kent Lodge, at Coniston.

> Lit.: A. Wilton, *The Life and Work of J.M.W. Turner* (London, 1979), no.555.

63 Joseph Mallord William Turner (1775–1851) *Swiss Valley*

Watercolour over some indications in graphite. 22.5 : 33.2 (sight)

Dating from the early 1840s, this scene has not yet been identified, but probably shows a view of Mont Blanc.

64 William Turner of Oxford (1789–1862) *At Ferry Hinksey*

Watercolours and bodycolour on blue paper. 27.5 : 46. Signed: *W. Turner/Oxford* and the date: *May 10th, 1842* written twice. Signed on the verso: *At Ferry Hinksey near Oxford, Study from natur(e)*

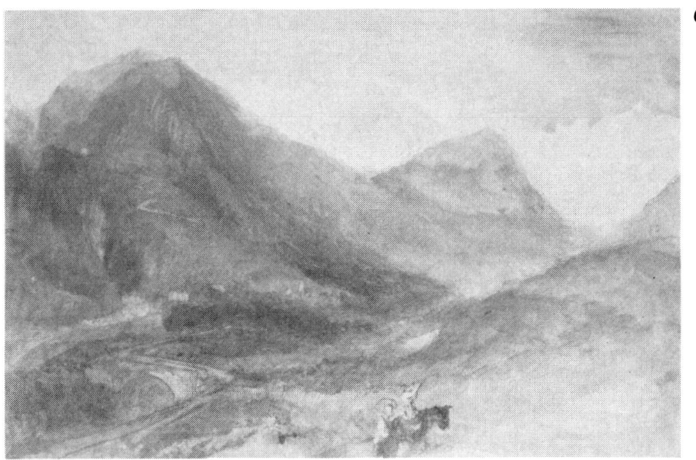

63

64

As a child William Turner lived at Shipton-on-Cherwell, near Woodstock. After training in London under John Varley and practising there for some years, he had a house in St. John Street, Oxford from 1831. He produced many precise watercolours depicting the ideal peace of the countryside around Oxford.

65 William Turner of Oxford (1789–1862) *Path through a Cornfield*
Watercolour and bodycolour over pencil on buff paper. 17.2 : 27.6. Inscribed on the verso: *Painted from Nature/In Dorchester field, Oxfordshire, Warborough, Benson & Ewelme/in the distance*
The handling in William Turner's later work becomes more free and less formal than before, as in this watercolour from 1845-50. The uncompromising composition, of a wide path in the foreground receding to strong horizontals on a high horizon, is typical of this period. The scene looks away from Dorchester toward the site of a British hill fort. Several studies exist in and around Dorchester and it is probable that Turner was attracted by its historic associations.

Lit.: see exhibition catalogue, *William Turner of Oxford* (Oxfordshire County Museums Service, 1984), p.69.

66 Willem van de Velde II (1633–1707) *Shipping Scene*
Pen and brown ink with grey wash. 15 : 28. Signed: *W.V.V.*
The ships appear to be flying Dutch flags, although the style suggests that it was probably drawn after the artist's move to England by 1672. The careful delineation of sky and sea produce a more than usually finished composition.

67 Edouard Vuillard (1868–1940) *Grey and White Houses*
Oil on panel. 27 : 17.5 (sight). Signed: *EV 92*
Grounded in the finest traditions of French painting, Vuillard was much influenced as a young painter by Sérusier and Bonnard and by Gauguin and the Nabis. His subjects were from Parisian life, displayed with forms and colours so strong that they acquire a certain monumentality. His intimiste paintings of the 1890s could be taken as Fauve works of about twenty years later. He was adept in the use of greys, creams and whites, as is shown here.

68 James Ward (1769–1859) *Sheep-shearing*
Oil on canvas. 69.6 : 90
The fine, rich handling of paint and the use of colourful and witty details are typical of Ward at this date. The painting was exhibited at the Royal Academy in 1846, no.354, as *Sheepshearing, taking off their clothes.*

Lit.: C.Reginald Grundy, *James Ward RA* (London, 1909), p.52, no.785.

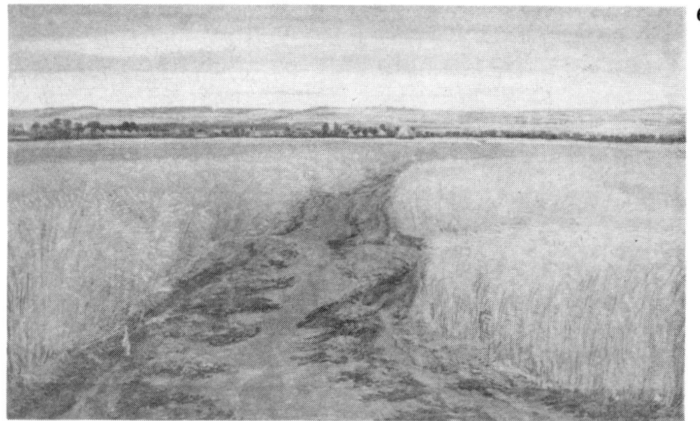

65

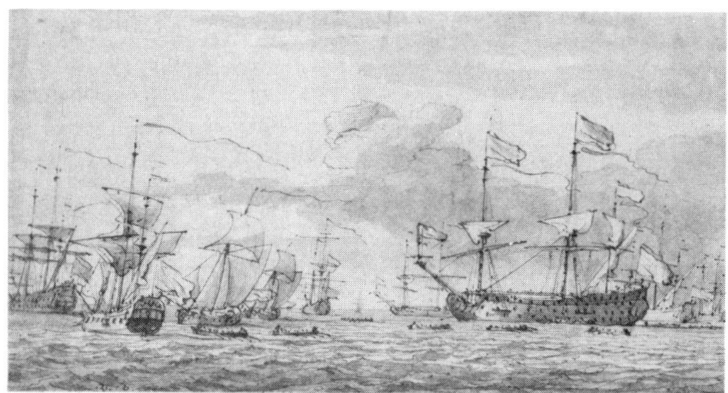

66

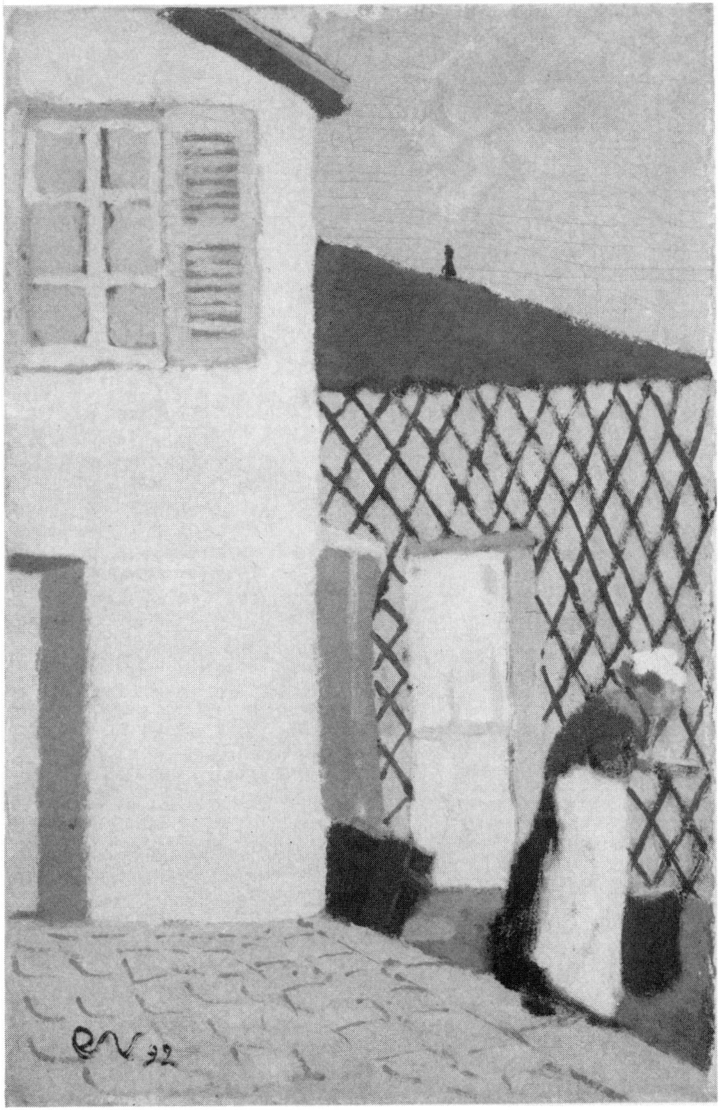

67

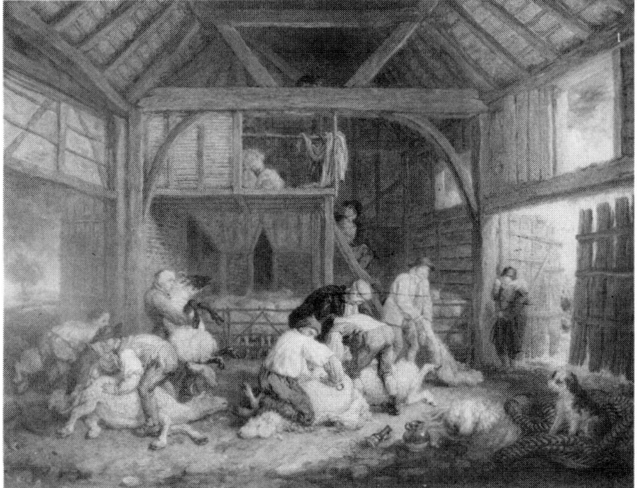

68

69 Sir David Wilkie (1785–1841) *The Spanish Mother*
  Oil on canvas. 99 : 124.5 (sight)

Wilkie spent eight months in Spain in 1827–28 and on his return was commissioned to paint several pictures on the basis of drawings he had made there. *The Spanish Mother* was commissioned in 1833 by Sir William Knighton, who was physician to the King and a great enthusiast of Wilkie's Spanish works. Preliminary drawings exist in the National Gallery of Scotland and the Ashmolean Museum, the latter version including, with other figures, the mother and child pose. The picture shows his interest in Correggio, as well as in Murillo whose works he had admired in Seville. *The Spanish Mother* was received with great acclaim at the 1834 Royal Academy, where artist and patron conspired to increase interest in it by keeping the details of the commission secret.

Lit.: Exhibition catalogue, *Sir David Wilkie of Scotland* (North Carolina Museum of Art, Raleigh, 1987), no.35.

70 Adam Willaerts (1577–1654) *Storm at Sea*
  Oil on panel. 47.5 : 113 (sight). Signed and dated: *A D Willarts.f/ 1649*

Although a native of Antwerp, who was trained in the Flemish tradition, the artist had moved to Utrecht by 1611, where he spent the remainder of his life. The crowded fish-market taking place on the beach became a favourite theme.

70

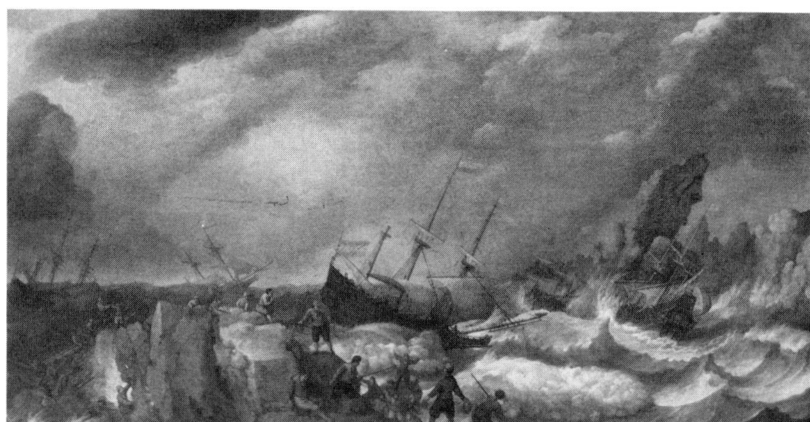

72

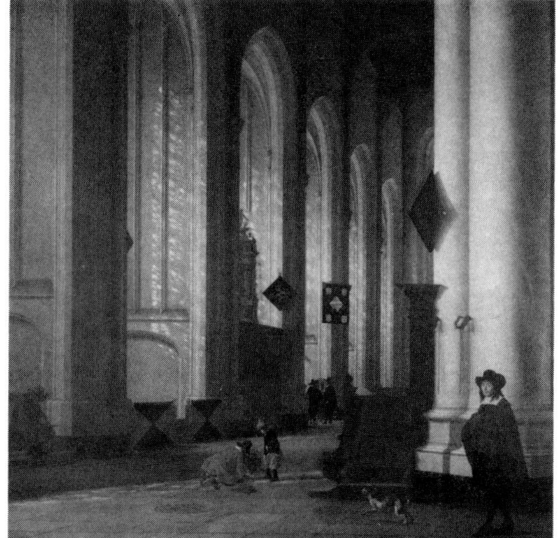

71

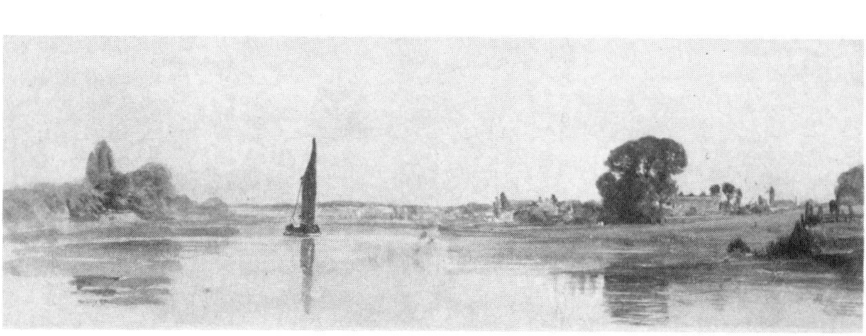

71 Peter de Wint (1784–1849) *View of the Thames near Broomhouse, Wandsworth*

Watercolour on two sheets of paper joined. 15.5 : 45.2

A prolific painter of closely-observed views in England and Wales, de Wint worked in watercolour out of doors. River scenery was a favourite theme, often treated in horizontal compositions, and in this de Wint was influenced by Dutch landscapes. The boldness of handling and the simplicity of effect are also characteristic in this charming Thames view in which the whiteness of the paper is exploited. De Wint's style followed a rapid development up to *c*.1810, but then changed little, so that his works are difficult to date.

72 Anthonie De Lorme (d. 1673) *The Interior of the Laurenskerk, Rotterdam*

Oil on canvas. 109 : 109. Signed *A. de. Lorme 1656*

A pupil of Jan van Vucht, de Lorme specialised in painting church interiors, particularly that of the Laurenskerk. A larger view is in the Hermitage, St. Petersburg.

Sculpture

1 William Theed the Younger (1804–91) *Narcissus*

Marble. 91 : 46 (including integral plinth). Signed on the plinth: *W. Theed./Fecit. Roma. 1848*

Theed studied and worked in Rome from 1826 to 1848, and established his reputation in England by sending work to the Royal Academy exhibitions. A major breakthrough came in his career when one of his mentors, John Gibson (a pupil of Canova) included Theed's designs among work by English sculptors in Rome sent to the Prince Consort as possible sculptures for Osborne House.

2 The Hon. Mrs Ann Seymour Damer (1748–1828) *Portrait Bust of Sarah Siddons (1755–1831)*

Terracotta. 54 high, incl. plinth of 11cm, 28 deep, 23.5 wide. Inscribed on the front in Greek. *ME^TIO MENH* and on the back, also in Greek: *ANNE SEYMOUR DAMER... 1794.*

Ann Seymour Damer exhibited this portrait bust at the Royal Academy in 1788. The rather blank expression and the inclination of the head are typical of her work, as are the stylised hair and the way the bust sits on a solid plinth, 'in the Grecian manner'. Damer aimed to make her subjects both life-like and classicising. Horace Walpole noted that she 'writes Latin like Pliny and is learning Greek' and was so impressed by her that he bequeathed her Strawberry Hill. Her achievements were rare for such an aristocratic woman in her day. Her accomplished sculpture includes heads of the Rivers Thames and Isis to decorate the bridge in Henley. Sarah Siddons had reached the peak of her acting career at this date. She had completed successful seasons at Drury Lane under the direction of David Garrick and had been playing Shakespearian roles for five years.

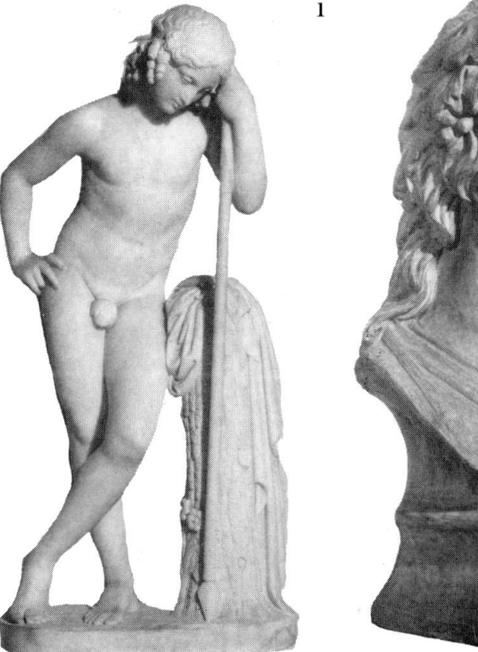

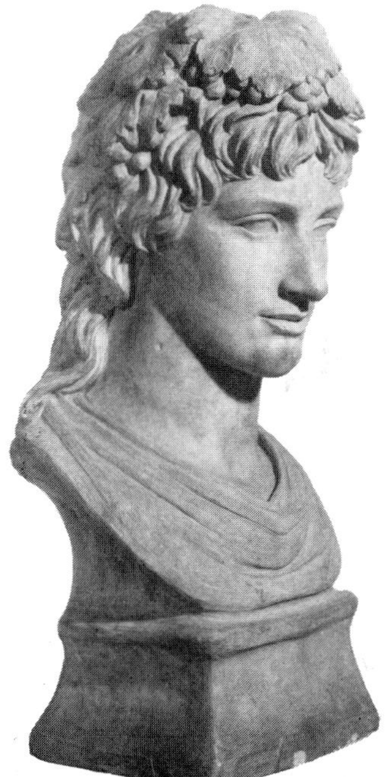

Mercers was established in Henley-on-Thames before 1827
and has grown to become a wide-ranging legal practice,
serving clients with many different legal requirements
throughout the South of England and further afield.

The firm, which has three offices in Henley-on-Thames
and Reading, provides a personal service to all clients, both
private and commercial. The Partners, most of whom came
from London firms, are all specialists in particular areas of
the law. We work in four main departments: Private Client,
Property, Company and Commercial and Litigation.

We have a particularly strong Private Client department
and connections with related advisers, fine art valuers,
leading accountants and appropriate members of the
London bar. We are well placed to advise clients on
heritage property, tax planning, settlements, wills and
trusts and establishment of charities.

We are a member firm of LawNet, the federation of
independent solicitors firms with members throughout
England and Wales, and are authorised by the Law Society
to conduct investment business.

We will be pleased to send you a copy of the firm's
brochure, which gives further details of the types of
work we conduct.

Exhibition sponsors

MERCERS

Solicitors

50 New Street	50A Bell Street	37 Minster Street
Henley-on-Thames	Henley-on-Thames	Reading
Oxfordshire	Oxfordshire	Berkshire
Tel 0491 572138	Tel 0491 572138	Tel 0734 599858
Fax 0491 572223	Fax 0491 579820	Fax 0734 507409